Oklahoma Test Preparation Book

Practice for OCCT
Grade 4

Harcourt School Publishers

www.harcourtschool.com

Copyright © by Harcourt, Inc.

All rights reserved. No part of this publication may be reproduced or transmitted in any form or by any means, electronic or mechanical, including photocopy, recording, or any information storage and retrieval system, without permission in writing from the publisher.

Requests for permission to make copies of any part of the work should be addressed to School Permissions and Copyrights, Harcourt, Inc., 6277 Sea Harbor Drive, Orlando, Florida 32887-6777. Fax: 407-345-2418.

HARCOURT and the Harcourt Logo are trademarks of Harcourt, Inc., registered in the United States of America and/or other jurisdictions.

Printed in the United States of America

ISBN 10 0-15-372861-2

ISBN 13 978-0-15-372861-7

If you have received these materials as examination copies free of charge, Harcourt School Publishers retains title to the materials and they may not be resold. Resale of examination copies is strictly prohibited and is illegal.

Possession of this publication in print format does not entitle users to convert this publication, or any portion of it, into electronic format.

---

6 7 8 9 10 1431 16 15 14 13 12 11

4500331216

Contents

Introduction 4
Get to Know the OCCT 5
Writing Prompt Rubric... 6
Composite Skills and Writer's Checklist..................... 8

Lesson

1: Context Clues 9
2: Main Idea and Details 11
3: Author's Purpose............ 13
4: Compare and Contrast ... 15
5: Narrative Response 17
6: Focus 19
7: Use Reference Sources.... 21
8: Root Words..................... 23
9: Characters, Setting, and Plot 25
10: Functional Response 27
11: Point of View 29
12: Drawing Conclusions.... 31
13: Similarities and Differences in Setting... 33
14: Cause and Effect 35
15: Biography 37
16: Multiple-Meaning Words and Idioms 39
17: Organization 41
18: Chronological Order 43

19: Punctuation and Capitalization 45
20: Creative Narrative 47
21: Author's Purpose.......... 49
22: Compare and Contrast...................... 51
23: Context Clues............... 53
24: Reference Information 55
25: Research 57
26: Conflict and Conflict Resolution 59
27: Fact and Opinion 61
28: Similarities and Differences in Characters................. 63
29: Cause and Effect 65
30: Informational Expository.................... 67

Practice Test 1................... 72
Practice Test 2................ 118
Practice Test 3................ 159

Introduction

What Is the OCCT?

The OCCT is a test of skills you learn in school.

The Reading section of the OCCT tests your reading skills. The test asks questions about stories, poems, or articles that you read. Most of the questions ask you to choose the correct answer.

The Writing section of the OCCT tests your writing skills. You will be asked to write a narrative, functional, informational, or research selection.

How to Prepare for the OCCT

This book will help you prepare for the OCCT. Lessons are included on the skills you will need for the Reading and Writing sections of the test. Three practice tests allow you to practice taking the OCCT Reading and Writing sections.

When you take the OCCT, make sure you have sharpened pencils. Sit quietly, and listen carefully to the directions. Sit up straight, and keep your eyes on your book. Read carefully. When you choose answers, fill the circles in all the way. Write your answers neatly.

Get to Know the OCCT

You will see special pictures and signs on the OCCT. This chart tells you what they mean.

What You Will See . . .	What It Means . . .
2 They went to the...	This number shows where a new paragraph begins in a selection. In poetry, lines 1, 5, 10, etc. are numbered.
GO ON ▶	This sign means the test keeps going on the next page.
STOP ●	This sign means you are at the end of the selection. This sign is also on both sections of the test. It means you are at the end of that section of the OCCT.

You will also see special words on the Reading section of the OCCT. This chart tells you what the words mean.

What You Will See . . .	What It Means . . .
Words in **bold**	Words in bold name a skill, such as **main idea**. Words in bold are also directions or questions.
Words in underline	An underlined word is a vocabulary word, such as emotion. Important words, such as best, same, and different help you choose the correct answer.

How Responses to Writing Prompts Are Scored on the OCCT

The Writing section of the OCCT asks you to write a narrative, functional, informational, or research selection. Your writing needs a main idea. It also needs a beginning, a middle, and an ending.

Analytic Scores

You will be scored on five characteristics of good writing. Writing selections are worth 4–1 points. These rubrics are used on the OCCT to assign the five analytic scores.

Score	Ideas and Development 30%
4	• The content is well suited for the audience and purpose • The main idea or thesis is clear • Ideas are fully developed and elaborated using details, examples, reasons, or evidence • The writer expresses an insightful perspective toward the topic
3	• The content is adequate for the audience and purpose • The main idea is evident but may lack clarity • Ideas are developed using some details, examples, reasons, and/or evidence • The writer sustains his/her perspective toward the topic throughout most of the composition
2	• The content is inconsistent with the audience and purpose • The main idea is not focused and leaves the reader with questions and making inferences to understand the main idea • Ideas are minimally developed with few details • May simply be a list of ideas • The writer has difficulty expressing his/her perspective toward the topic
1	• The content is irrelevant to the audience and purpose • The composition lacks a central idea • Ideas lack development or may be repetitive • The writer has little or no perspective on the topic

Score	Organization, Unity, and Coherence 25%
4	• Introduction engages the reader • Sustained or consistent focus on the topic • Logical and appropriate sequencing and balanced with smooth, effective transitions • Order and structure are strong and move the reader through the text • Conclusion is satisfying
3	• Evident introduction to the topic • Adequate focus • Adequate sequencing • Stays on topic with little digression • Uses limited but effective transitions • Order and structure are present • Conclusion is appropriate
2	• May lack a clear organizational structure • Weak evidence of unity • Little or limited sequencing and/or transitions • Details may be randomly placed
1	• Lacks logical direction • No evidence of organizational structure

Score	Word Choice 15%
4	- Appropriate word choice which conveys the correct meaning and appeals to the audience in an interesting, precise, and natural way - The writing may be characterized by, but not limited to: lively verbs, vivid nouns, imaginative adjectives, figurative language, and dialogue - No vague, overused, repetitive language is used (*a lot, great, very, really*)
3	- Words generally convey the intended message - The writer uses a variety of words that are appropriate but do not necessarily energize the writing - The writing may be characterized by: attempts at figurative language and dialogue, some use of lively verbs, vivid nouns, and imaginative adjectives, and few vague, overused, and repetitive words.
2	- Word choice lacks precision and variety or may be inappropriate to the audience and purpose - May be simplistic and/or vague - Relies on overused or vague language (*a lot, great, very, really*) - Few attempts at figurative language and dialogue - Word choice is unimaginative and colorless with images that are unclear or absent
1	- Word choice indicates an extremely limited or inaccurate vocabulary - No attempts at figurative language - General, vague words that fail to communicate meaning - Text may be too short to demonstrate variety

Score	Sentences and Paragraphs 15%
4	- Writing clearly demonstrates appropriate sentence structure - Writing has few or no run-on or fragment errors - Writing has a rich variety of sentence structure, types, and lengths - Ideas are organized into paragraphs that blend into larger text - Evidence of appropriate paragraphing
3	- Writing adequately demonstrates appropriate sentence structure - Writing may contain a small number of run-on or fragment errors that do not interfere with fluency - Writing has adequate variety of sentence structure - Ideas may be organized into paragraphs
2	- Writing demonstrates lack of control in sentence structure - Writing contains errors such as run-ons and fragments that interfere with fluency - Writing has limited variety of sentence structure - Writing may show little or no attempt at paragraphing
1	- Inappropriate sentence structure - Many errors in structure (run-ons, fragments) - No variety in structure - No attempt at paragraphing

Score	Grammar, Usage, and Mechanics 15%
4	• The writer demonstrates appropriate use of correct: spelling, punctuation, capitalization, grammar, and usage • Errors are minor and do not affect readability
3	• The writer demonstrates appropriate use of correct: spelling, punctuation, capitalization, grammar, and usage • Errors may be more noticeable but do not significantly affect readability
2	• The writer demonstrates appropriate use of correct: spelling, punctuation, capitalization, grammar, and usage • Errors may be distracting and interfere with readability
1	• The writer demonstrates appropriate use of correct: spelling, punctuation, capitalization, grammar, and usage • Errors are numerous and severely impede readability

Composite Score

Your composite score is worth 6–1. The percentages given to each analytic score are provided in the table below.

Percentage	Analytic Score Category
30%	Ideas and Development
25%	Organization, Unity, and Coherence
15%	Word Choice
15%	Sentences and Paragraphs
15%	Grammar, Usage, and Mechanics

Writer's Checklist

Look at the checklist below before you begin writing.

Focus	Support
_____ Make the main idea of your writing clear to your readers. _____ Stick to the topic.	_____ Choose words to help readers understand your topic. _____ Answer the prompt completely. _____ Give enough information to make your ideas clear.
Organization	**Conventions**
_____ Use connecting words to join your ideas. _____ Include details to support your main idea. _____ Include a clear beginning, middle, and end.	_____ Punctuate your sentences correctly. _____ Write in complete sentences. _____ Begin each sentence and every proper noun with a capital letter. _____ Check your spelling.

LESSON 1

OCCT Test Preparation

Context Clues

When you see an unfamiliar word in a story, read nearby words, phrases, sentences, and paragraphs to find its meaning. This is called using **context clues.** Context clues give you hints about the word's meaning. They can also help you figure out the meaning of a word that has more than one meaning. Sometimes context clues can give you a **definition** of the word.

Jamie's favorite kind of sled is a *toboggan.*

You can guess that a *toboggan* is a kind of sled.

Other times context clues can give you a **general idea** about the meaning of the word.

Ms. Ruiz carefully *inspected* the floor for her missing earring.

You can guess that *inspected* means "searched."

Read the selection below. Then answer the question that follows.

Making Dinner

Carmen's father asked her to help him make dinner. First, she prepared the vegetables. She filled the sink with water. Next, she scrubbed the potatoes and carrots until they were spotless. Then her father cut them into small pieces. Carmen put the carrots and potatoes into a large bowl. Finally, Carmen's father showed her how to make a sauce. They mixed oil and spices together. She poured the sauce over the vegetables. Now the vegetables were ready to be roasted.

1

What does the word scrubbed mean as it is used in this story?

A divided
B cleaned
C examined
D cooked

OCCT PASS 1.1 Use context clues

Name: Elijah Ledbetter   Date: _____

Independent Practice

Read the selection below. Then answer the questions that follow.

Rashan's Poem

1   "Good morning, class," said Mr. Calvin. "Today is the last day to hand in poems for the poetry contest. If you wish to enter a poem, leave it on my desk by the end of the day."

2   Rashan thought about the poem he had written. It was about his pet frog, and it was the best he had ever written. Rashan was so excited that he could not concentrate on his schoolwork. He reminded himself to take his poem out of his bag before he went home.

3   The bell rang at the end of the day. Rashan grabbed his bag and raced out of the room. Then, he remembered his poem! He hastened back to the room, hoping to catch Mr. Calvin before he left. He burrowed through his bag, but his digging turned up nothing.

4   Rashan had an idea. Even though his poem had vanished from his bag, it had not disappeared from his memory. He took out a tablet and began to write.

2

Which words have almost the same meaning as concentrate?

A   start over
B   learn from
C   think about ✓
D   figure out

3

What does the word hastened mean as it is used in this story?

A   rushed ✓
B   crawled
C   sneaked
D   wandered

4

We know that burrowed has to do with digging because

A   we learn about Rashan's bag.
B   digging is used in the same sentence. ✓
C   nothing is used in the same sentence.
D   we learn that the poem is gone.

Lesson 2: Main Idea and Details

The **main idea** of a passage is the most important idea. The main idea tells you what the passage is mostly about.
- Sometimes one sentence states the main idea. The main idea sentence is usually at the beginning of a paragraph.
- Sometimes you will have to discover the main idea.
- To find a main idea that is not stated, look at details for clues.

Details support or tell more about the main idea. They may give facts about the topic. Details may also tell you the order in which events happen in a story. To find out the order of events in a story, look for clue words such as *before, first, next, then, after,* or *finally.*

Read the selection below. Then answer the question that follows.

The Interesting Life of the Sea Otter

Sea otters are different from most other animals that live in the ocean. Sea otters have thicker fur than any other marine animal. This fur keeps them warm in cold ocean water. Sea otters are also one of the few animals that can use tools. Sea otters use rocks to smash open shells while feeding. They also tie long pieces of seaweed around their bodies. The seaweed keeps the otters from floating away in a strong current.

---

1. This selection is <u>mostly</u> about

A. how sea otters stay warm in the water.
B. why sea otters are unusual animals.
C. why sea otters use rocks to open shells.
D. why sea otters tie seaweed around their bodies.

OCCT *PASS* 3.3.a. Recognize main idea

Name: Elijah Ledbetter   Date: _____

Independent Practice

Read the selection below. Then answer the questions that follow.

Amelia Earhart

1   Amelia Earhart was a famous airplane pilot. She wanted to do things that no one had done before. She set many records for flying.

2   Earhart was born in 1897 and grew up with a love for flying. She went to air shows as a child. She watched pilots perform amazing tricks in the air. She worked many different jobs. Finally, she saved enough money to buy her own airplane.

3   Earhart became famous for flying when she was a young woman. In 1928 Earhart was asked to join a crew that flew across the Atlantic Ocean. Earhart became well-known after this trip.

4   Earhart set many records as a pilot. In 1932 she flew across the Atlantic Ocean by herself. She was the first woman to make the trip alone. A few years later, she was the first person to fly alone across the Pacific Ocean.

5   Amelia Earhart wanted to help other women become interested in flying. She wrote about flying for a famous women's magazine. She also started a networking group for women pilots. Earhart's love of flying brought her great success.

2 This story is <u>mostly</u> about

A the airplane tricks that Amelia Earhart performed in the air.

B how Amelia Earhart helped other women pilots.

C Amelia Earhart's activities as an airplane pilot.

D how Amelia Earhart became interested in flying.

3 Which details support the idea that Amelia Earhart wanted other women to fly?

A She was born in 1897 and grew up to love flying.

B She watched many pilots perform at air shows.

C She set many records as a well-known female pilot.

D She wrote about flying and started a networking group.

OCCT Test Preparation — Lesson 2

LESSON 3: Author's Purpose

Authors have different **purposes**, or *reasons* for writing. An author will sometimes state his or her purpose in the text. Often, you must discover the author's purpose by looking for clues in the text. The chart below lists three common purposes.

Author's Purpose	Type of Writing	Clues in the Text
To entertain	fiction	• tells a story • includes characters
To inform	nonfiction	• gives facts • does not give opinions
To persuade	nonfiction	• tells you what to think or do • often uses *you, your, must, should,* or *need to*

Read the selection below. Then answer the question that follows.

Chimpanzees

A chimpanzee is a type of monkey that lives in many countries in Africa. Chimpanzees live in areas that have warm weather all year. They grow to be about four feet tall. Long black hair covers their bodies. Chimpanzees can walk on all four legs or on their two back legs. They eat mostly fruits, insects, and nuts, and they sometimes eat meat.

1. The author wrote this selection mainly to

A teach the reader a lesson about taking care of animals.

B persuade the reader to learn more about chimpanzees.

C inform the reader about a certain kind of monkey.

D entertain the reader with an amusing story about monkeys.

OCCT *PASS* 4.2.b. Identify purpose of text

Name: Elijah Ledbetter   Date: _____

Independent Practice

Read the selection below. Then answer the questions that follow.

Getting Ready for Winter

1   David was helping his grandparents prepare their house for the winter. The last few nights had been very cold. In the morning, he had seen frost sparkling on the grass and plants outside. It was time to get the house ready for the long months of cold weather.

2   First, David's grandmother took the screens out of the windows. In the summer, the screens allowed cool breezes into the house. David helped replace the screens with thick panes of glass. These would keep out the wind, rain, and snow.

3   Then, David's grandfather asked David to help him carry some tables and chairs out to the shed. The family often ate meals outside in the summer during the nice weather. In the winter, the furniture would be safe and dry in the shed.

4   David opened the shed door and turned on the light. Then, he heard a chirping sound. He saw a bird building a warm nest high up on a shelf. The bird had a piece of straw in its shiny orange beak. David smiled—his family was not the only one getting ready for winter.

2 The author wrote this selection mainly to

A persuade readers to start preparing for winter.
B entertain readers by telling an interesting story.
C teach readers how to prepare a house for winter.
D inform readers about different types of birds' nests.

3 The author describes the bird's nest to

A make readers laugh at the bird's unusual winter nest.
B give readers information about a certain type of bird.
C persuade readers that they should care for wild animals.
D show readers that the bird was also preparing for winter.

OCCT Test Preparation — Lesson 3

LESSON 4: Compare and Contrast

To **compare** means to tell how things are alike. To **contrast** means to tell how things are different. When you read a story, you can compare and contrast characters, places, and events.

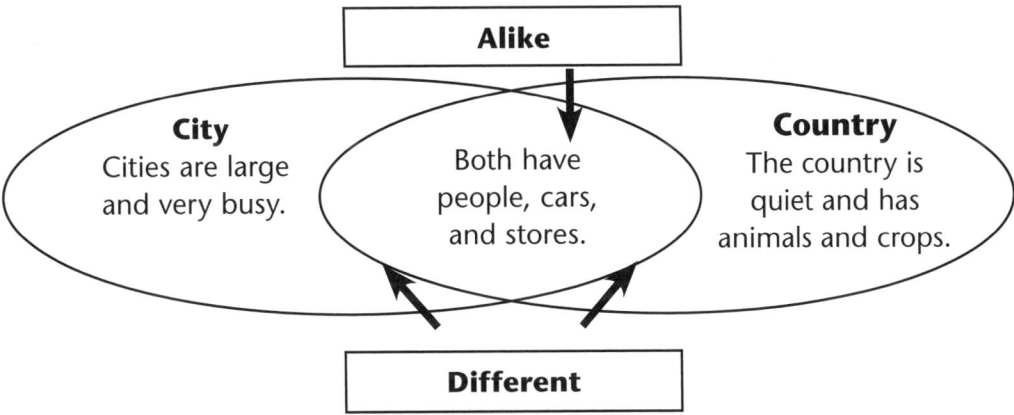

Read the selection below. Then answer the question that follows.

1   Today was Lucy's last day visiting her aunt. At breakfast, Lucy sat quietly and stared at her food. She was unable to enjoy herself because she didn't want to go home.

2   Just then, Lucy's aunt surprised her. She told Lucy that they were going to celebrate their last day together. They were going on a hike, and they would take a picnic lunch. Now, Lucy felt excited instead of sad. She knew that this would be a special day.

1 How did Lucy change her mind about her last day?

A At first she felt bored, but then she had fun.

B At first she was thrilled, but then she felt bored.

C At first she was upset, but then she enjoyed the day.

D At first she felt happy, but then she wanted to go home early.

OCCT *PASS* 3.4.b Compare and contrast

Name _____   Date _____

Independent Practice

Read the selection below. Then answer the questions that follow.

The Rainy Day

1   Derek rolled over and looked out his bedroom window. It was raining heavily. He jumped out of bed and cheered. He ran to his other window and looked out at the rain again. It seemed as though it would keep raining for a long time. Derek grinned with delight.

2   Derek went over to his bookcase, which was jammed full with books. He chose a thick book he had not read yet. Then, he piled his pillows on his bed so that he could lean against them. Finally, Derek crawled back under his blanket and began to read.

3   On the other side of the house, Derek's sister, Janelle, also woke up and looked out her window. When she saw the raindrops running down her windowpane, she frowned. She looked at her baseball glove and bat leaning against the wall and knew that she would not be able to use them today. She pulled the covers up over her head.

4   Suddenly, Derek thought of his sister. He knew that to her, a rainy day was like a party that had been canceled. He decided to try to brighten her day.

2

In what way do Derek and Janelle feel <u>differently</u> about rainy days?

A Derek is bored on rainy days, but Janelle finds them exciting.
B Derek looks forward to rainy days, but Janelle dislikes them.
C Derek likes rainy days best, and Janelle agrees with him.
D Derek thinks rainy days are fine, but Janelle loves them.

3

In this story, a rainy day is compared to a canceled party because <u>both</u> are

A jamming.
B surprising.
C grinning.
D disappointing.

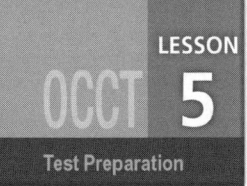

LESSON 5: Narrative Response

Today you will write a narrative on an assigned topic. Your writing will be scored on how fully you develop the topic and on how well you organize and express your ideas. Your composition will be scored by trained readers. As you work, keep in mind these three stages of the writing process:

- **Planning:** Take time to plan your writing by listing, outlining, or organizing your ideas in the space provided.

- **Writing:** Write about the topic in a clear and logical manner in the space provided. Make sure your composition is as complete as possible. Be sure to include a beginning, middle, and ending for your composition.

- **Editing/Revising:** Take time to reread what you have written, and decide if you need to add more details or change the organization of your composition. At the same time, look for and correct any errors in grammar, punctuation, capitalization, and spelling. You may use the *Writer's Checklist* on page 8 of this book to help you revise your writing.

> Think about a place you enjoy visiting. What is special about it? How do you feel when you are there? Why is this place enjoyable for you?

OCCT *PASS* Writing 2.4.   Write informational pieces with multiple paragraphs

Name _____ Date _____

Independent Practice

Read the writing prompt below. Then complete the graphic organizer and write a narrative response.

Which of the four seasons of the year is your favorite? Why?

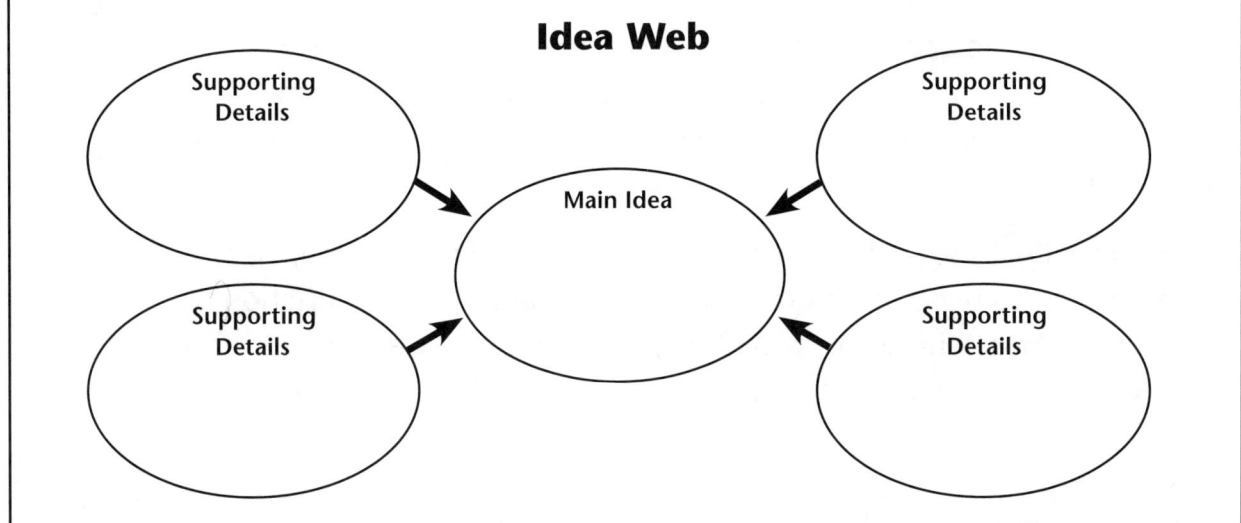

Idea Web

_____
_____
_____
_____
_____
_____
_____
_____
_____
_____

OCCT Lesson 6 — Focus

When you read a selection, it is important to tell the difference between **important details** and **unimportant details**. Paying attention to important and unimportant details is called **focus**. It is important to stay focused when you read. While you read, think about the selection's main idea. Then ask yourself, "Does this detail support the main idea?" Staying focused while you read will help you become a better reader and test taker.

Read the selection below. Then answer the question that follows.

The Mouse in the Woods

Yesterday was a beautiful day, so Aunt Isabel and I walked in the woods. We saw many people walking dogs. I wished that I had a pet. My aunt and I sat in a shady spot, and we ate our picnic lunch. Suddenly, I noticed some movement in a small pile of leaves. Aunt Isabel was wearing her brightly colored orange sweater. Out of curiosity, I pulled back the leaves carefully, and I found a mouse! Aunt Isabel said that it was not a wild mouse, so it must be a lost pet. We took it home, and we are trying to find its owner.

---

1. Which sentence contains a detail that is <u>unimportant</u> to the story?

A Yesterday was a beautiful day, so Aunt Isabel and I walked in the woods.

B My aunt and I sat in a shady spot, and we ate our picnic lunch.

C Aunt Isabel was wearing her brightly colored orange sweater.

D Out of curiosity, I pulled back the leaves carefully, and I found a mouse!

OCCT PASS 3.3.a. Recognize supporting details

Name _____ Date _____

Independent Practice

Read the selection below. Then answer the questions that follow.

Haruki's Trip

1 Haruki and his family were going to visit his grandparents. Haruki's father and brother were busy packing the car. They asked him to help. Haruki shook his head and continued playing. Haruki's favorite class in school is math.

2 Haruki quickly became bored in the car. He started singing one of his favorite songs. His brother, Yoshi, was working on an important drawing for a school project. Yoshi glared at him and said he couldn't draw while Haruki was singing. Haruki asked Yoshi whether he wanted to play a game. Yoshi only glared angrily at him again.

3 Haruki's father heard the argument. He told Haruki that he should have planned ahead for the trip. Haruki knew that his father was right. Then Yoshi gave him some drawing paper and pencils. Haruki thanked him and promised that he would help pack for their next trip.

2 Which sentence contains a detail that is <u>unimportant</u> to the story?

A Haruki's favorite class in school is math.
B He started singing one of his favorite songs.
C Yoshi only glared angrily at him again.
D Haruki's father heard the argument.

3 How is paragraph 1 related to the rest of the story?

A Haruki refuses to help pack, so Yoshi glares at him.
B Haruki doesn't pack anything, so he is bored in the car.
C Haruki explains that his favorite class in school is math.
D Haruki's brother and father are packing, so Haruki sings.

LESSON 7: Use Reference Sources

Reference sources can show you information in many ways. The table below lists a few reference sources and the types of information they contain.

Source	Purpose	Type of Information
Almanac	gives facts about places, sports, weather, and events	text, charts
Atlas	shows where places are located	maps
Dictionary	gives word meanings	text
Thesaurus	lists words with the same meaning	text
Encyclopedia	gives information on topics	text, maps, charts, photographs

You can see that along with text, many reference sources include maps, charts, and photographs. Pay special attention to reference sources to find the information you need.

Look at the selection below. Then answer the question that follows.

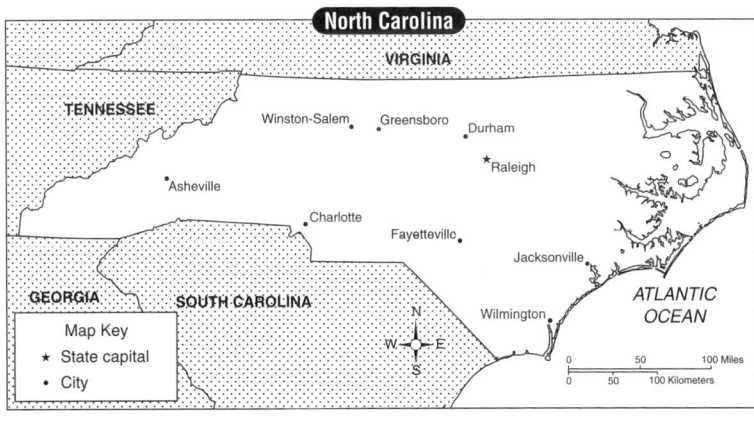

1 Based on the map, which city is the state capital?

A Asheville

B Charlotte

C Raleigh

D Fayetteville

OCCT *PASS* 5.1.a. Understand the organization and access information from a variety of sources

Independent Practice

Read the selection below. Then answer the questions that follow.

jam–jungle

jam *noun*
1. a spread made of crushed fruit: *He spreads strawberry jam on his bread.*
verb
2a. to pack something tightly: *He jammed his clothes into his drawer.*
2b. to make something become stuck: *She jammed the machine and made it stop working.*

jaw *noun*
1. the part of the face under the mouth: *She rested her jaw in her hand.*

jingle *noun*
1. a short song that is easy to remember: *She sang the jingle that she heard on the radio.*
verb
2. to make a tinkling sound: *The coins jingled in her pocket.*

jungle *noun*
1. a wild area filled with tropical plants and trees: *Monkeys live in the jungle.*
2. something that is confusing or messy: *The closet was a jungle of old toys.*

2 Based on its dictionary entry, what is one meaning of the word **jingle**?

A the part of the face under the mouth
B to make something become stuck
C a short song that is easy to remember
D to pack something tightly

3 Based on the dictionary entries, which word is a kind of food?

A jingle
B jungle
C jaw
D jam

LESSON 8 — Root Words

Test Preparation

A word may have several parts. A **root word**, or **root**, is the basic word part that gives the word meaning. A **prefix** is a word part added to the beginning of a word. A **suffix** is a word part added to the end of a word.

This chart shows some frequently used prefixes and suffixes.

Prefix	Meaning	Root	Word
un-	not	able	unable
re-	again, back	write	rewrite
pre-	before	view	preview
dis-	not, opposite	agree	disagree

Suffix	Meaning	Root	Word
-able	can be, having	comfort	comfortable
-er	a person who	teach	teacher
-less	without, not	harm	harmless
-ness	being or having that condition	happy	happiness

Read the selection below. Then answer the question that follows.

The Announcement

Tyler stood <u>motionless</u> in the center of the room. It was as if she were frozen, and suddenly she felt like crying. Her mother had announced that she was taking a new job in Miami. It was a good job, but the family would have to move. Tyler felt uncertain about moving to such a big city. She would miss all her friends and neighbors. She was sure of one thing. Her mom needed her help.

---

1 What does the word <u>motionless</u> mean?

A not moving *(circled)*
B actively moving
C the act of moving
D moving again

OCCT *PASS* 1.2.b. Identify root words

Name _____ Date _____

Independent Practice

Read the selection below. Then answer the questions that follow.

Earning Power

1 Maybe you are saving for a new CD. Maybe you want to buy a birthday gift for someone. Whatever the reason, many young people enjoy finding ways to make money.

2 A job is a big responsibility. If you promise to do something, can you keep that promise? Being dependable is a big part of earning money.

3 Think about how much time you can give to a job. Will you have enough time for schoolwork and your family?

4 Do you like animals? You could start a pet care service. Often, people need someone to check on their cats, birds, and fish while they're away.

5 If you like to be outside, you might be interested in doing yard work. People always need leaves raked during the fall.

6 Small jobs like these give you an idea of what it's like to work and earn your own money. Need some business advice? Here are some important things to remember:

7 Treat your customers with honesty and respect. If your customers believe that you've mistreated them or acted unfairly, they won't hire you again.

8 Tell your parents or guardians. For example, if you are walking a neighbor's pet, tell your parents or guardians the person's name and where you will be.

9 Think like a business manager. Family members can help you decide how much to charge your customers. They can also help you think of ways to advertise your business.

10 Whether you work alone or work with friends, earning your own money can be rewarding and fun!

2

If depend means "trust," what does dependable mean?

A can trust again
B can be trusted
C without trust
D full of trust

3

If treat means "to care for," what does mistreat mean?

A treat badly
B treat again
C treat first
D treat last

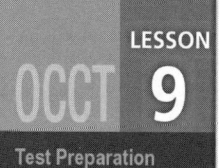

LESSON 9: Characters, Setting, and Plot

Characters, setting, and **plot** are the parts of a story. These parts work together to shape a story. The chart below describes the three parts of a story.

Characters	Setting	Plot
• People or animals in a story • Usually faced with a problem that they must solve	• Where a story takes place • When a story takes place	• Series of events in a story • Usually includes a main problem, which is often solved at the end of the story

Read the selection below. Then answer the question that follows.

A New House

1 Salvador's parents are going to build a new house. Today, workers will tear down the old house and take it away. Then, a new house will be built on the same spot. Salvador's family and friends gather outside to watch the big event.

2 "Salvador," his father says, "this is an exciting day, but I am also sad to see our old house go. We spent many happy years in that house." Salvador has an idea. He runs to the car and comes back with drawing paper and a pencil. He will make sure that his father always remembers their old house.

1 How does Salvador's father feel in the story?

A He is upset at the thought of the old house's being torn down.

B He believes that the workers will do a poor job on the old house.

C He is angry that Salvador wants to draw a picture of the old house.

D He wishes that his family and friends were there with him.

OCCT PASS 4.2.a. Identify/explain plot structure

Independent Practice

Read the selection below. Then answer the questions that follow.

After the Storm

1. The storm lasted almost all weekend. As Chen lay in bed at night, she could hear the rain pounding against her window. When she looked outside in the morning, the trees were bending and twisting in the wind like dancers. Chen and her family stayed inside, playing games and reading books.

2. After two days, the storm finally stopped. Chen's mother looked outside and sighed at the mess in the yard. The grass was covered by a thick layer of twigs and leaves. She asked Chen to help her clean the yard.

3. Chen also sighed because she had just finished setting up the checkerboard for a game. She put on her coat and went outside to help her mother. She worked slowly, removing only one small branch at a time. Chen looked hopefully at the sky, but no clouds were in sight.

4. "Chen, you'll never win the game if you don't speed up," her mother said with a smile. "My pile is already twice as big as yours, and the person with the biggest pile wins!" Chen laughed and filled her arms with as many twigs as she could hold. She realized that she was not sad that the storm had ended.

2 What problem does Chen have in the story?

A She is sad because she must stay inside during the storm.

B She wants to play checkers rather than clean the yard.

C She is upset that her yard is covered with branches.

D She worries that another storm is going to begin.

3 How is the problem solved?

A Chen's mother makes a game out of cleaning the yard.

B Chen's mother tells her that she may stay inside if she wishes.

C Chen's mother promises to play checkers when they finish.

D Chen's mother asks the neighbors to help them clean the yard.

LESSON 10: Functional Response

A lot of writing is functional. To-do lists, recipes, letters, maps, and advertisements are examples of functional writing. **Functional writing** serves a purpose.

Functional writing should be well organized. The main idea should come first. Supporting ideas should follow the main idea.

Today you will write a functional response on an assigned topic. Your writing will be scored on how fully you develop the topic and how well you organize and express your ideas. Your composition will be scored by trained readers. As you work, keep in mind these three stages of the writing process:

- **Planning:** Take time to plan your writing by listing, outlining, or organizing your ideas in the space provided.

- **Writing:** Write about the topic in a clear and logical manner in the space provided. Make sure your composition is as complete as possible. Be sure to include a beginning, middle, and ending for your composition.

- **Editing/Revising:** Take time to reread what you have written, and decide if you need to add more details or change the organization of your composition. At the same time, look for and correct any errors in grammar, punctuation, capitalization, and spelling. You may use the *Writer's Checklist* on page 8 of this book to help you revise your writing.

> **Write a letter to a friend whom you have not seen in a long time. Tell your friend how you are and explain why. Use proper letter formatting.**

OCCT PASS Writing 2.3. Write a personal letter

Name _____ Date _____

Independent Practice

Read the writing prompt below. Then complete the graphic organizer and write a functional response.

Write an advertisement for a healthy snack. Remember, the main idea is that this is a healthy snack to eat. What sort of supporting details would be useful in this advertisement?

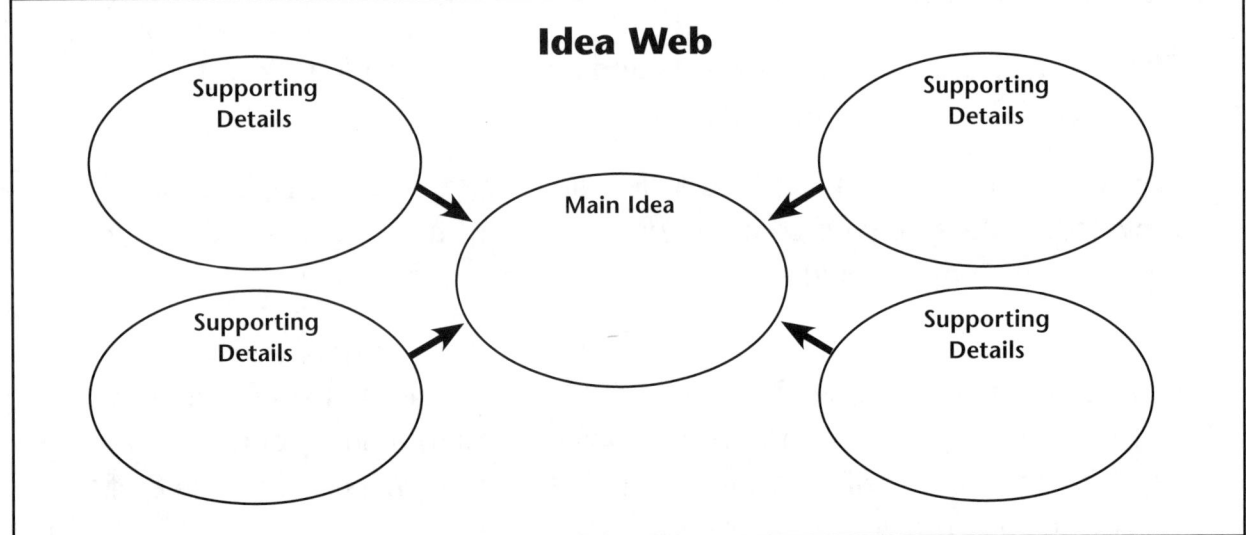

OCCT Test Preparation — Page 28 — Lesson 10

LESSON 11: Point of View

Authors tell their stories through different characters or through themselves. **Point of view** is the term we use to describe *who* or *what* is telling the story. It is important to understand point of view while reading so that you can understand what kinds of information might be left out. The table below shows different points of view. Another name for point of view is *person*.

Point of View	Words Used to Show Point of View	Example
First person	I, my, me, mine, her, him, we, us	*I* zipped down the hill on *my* scooter.
Second person	you, yours	*You* should be careful when holding an egg.
Third person	he, his, him, she, hers, her, they, their, theirs, them, it, its, or names	*They* were so excited to visit *their* grandparents. *Jenny* was sad to see *Uncle Ron* go back home.

Read the selection below. Then answer the question that follows.

Microscopes and Telescopes

1. Do you want to look at something tiny? You can use a microscope.
2. Most microscopes use glass lenses to make things look bigger. Under a microscope, you can see even tiny cells.
3. The first microscopes were made in the Netherlands around 1600.
4. What if you want to see something that's far away? Then your best bet is a telescope. Telescopes use lenses to gather light from faraway objects.
5. Galileo used the telescope that he made in 1609. He looked at the stars and planets. He learned that the moon has mountains.

1 We know that this article is written in the second person because it uses

A the pronoun *I*.
B the pronoun *he*.
C the pronoun *you*.
D the pronoun *us*.

OCCT PASS 4.1.a. Identify the defining characteristics of literary genres and forms

Name _____ Date _____

Independent Practice

Read the selection below. Then answer the questions that follow.

A Bedtime Story

1 It was time for bed, but Janet and Marcus were not ready to sleep yet. They wanted to hear a bedtime story. Their father, Mr. Blum, asked them what story they wanted to hear.

2 "It should be about an exciting race," said Janet.

3 "And a knight that fights monsters," added Marcus.

4 "Can there also be a volcano erupting?" asked Janet.

5 Mr. Blum thought for a while. How could he fit all those things into one story? Then he had an idea.

6 "Once upon a time, Janet and Marcus took a trip to the art museum. They saw many pictures. One was about an exciting race. Another showed a knight who was fighting dragons. A third picture showed an erupting volcano. Janet and Marcus liked the museum very much. They talked about the different paintings until they fell asleep." Mr. Blum stopped. He wanted to see what the children thought of his story.

7 It was too late. They were both sound asleep.

2 In which point of view is paragraph 1 written?

A first person
B third person
C second person
D no person

3 Paragraph 7 is written in the third person because it uses

A the word they.
B pictures about the story.
C the words his and hers.
D the children's names.

4 Why does the author quote the exact words that Janet and Marcus say?

A to tell what he really saw
B to show that Janet and Marcus are angry
C to suggest that Mr. Blum tells too many stories
D to explain the main parts of a good bedtime story

OCCT Test Preparation   Lesson 11

LESSON 12: Drawing Conclusions

Many questions ask you to draw conclusions. **Drawing conclusions** means adding ideas from a story to things you already know in order to *make a judgment.* Before you read, think about what you already know about the subject of the story. As you read, use what you already know and add it to what you read. Then you will be able to draw a conclusion.

Read the selection below. Then answer the question that follows.

A Speech

1   Sydney was nervous. Her hands were shaking, and her stomach felt a little funny. She really wanted this day to be over as soon as possible. She did not want to speak in front of the class today. Sydney grabbed her coat and said goodbye to her mother.

2   She walked down the street and followed the trail through Springhill Park. The warm air and bright sun made her feel good. Also, she could think more clearly outdoors. Sydney soon found herself practicing her speech. As she walked, she thought of new things to say and new ways to say them. Ideas were jumping into her head.

3   By the time school was in view, she had an exciting new plan for her speech. Finally, she hurried to her class to prepare for her presentation.

---

1 From paragraph 2, we can conclude that Sydney

A wanted to go home.
B thought her speech was dull.
C enjoyed being outdoors.
D found her friends at the park.

OCCT *PASS* 3.2.c. Draw conclusions about characters

Name _____   Date _____

Independent Practice

Read the selection below. Then answer the questions that follow.

Marisol's Lucky Saturday

1   Saturday is Marisol's favorite day. She and her mother always get up early and walk to the park. They bring Sparkle, Marisol's dog with them. Marisol and her mother play catch with Sparkle. Marisol looks forward to Saturday all week.

2   This week, Marisol's plans for Saturday change. Her mother must leave town. Marisol will spend Saturday afternoon with her older cousin, Janet. Janet does not like to play catch. She likes indoor games.

3   This Saturday begins badly. When Marisol wakes up, it is pouring rain. Later, she spills her cereal on the floor. By the time Janet comes over at noon, Marisol is fed up with this Saturday. She is ready to cry.

4   Things change when Janet teaches her to play a new game. Marisol begins to feel better when she beats Janet on her third try. When her mother gets home later in the evening, Marisol tells her all about the new game.

2 From paragraph 1, we can conclude that Marisol

A   walks her dog without her mother.
B   visits her cousin, Janet.
C   changes her plans suddenly.
D   looks forward to Saturday all week.

3 What can we conclude about Marisol and Janet?

A   They both like to play catch.
B   They are very different people.
C   They change their minds a lot.
D   They both like to walk the dog.

4 In paragraph 3, Marisol is ready to cry. We can conclude that she

A   is upset by the change in plans, the rain, and spilling her cereal.
B   wants her mother to take her on her trip out of town.
C   tries to hide her feelings from her cousin, Janet.
D   looks forward to playing a new game with her cousin.

LESSON 13 Similarities and Differences in Setting

When settings are **similar** to each other, they are alike. When settings are **different** from each other, they are not alike. To find similarities and differences, think about where and when the story takes place.

Settings can change during the story. Think about what the setting is at the beginning of the story and at the end of the story. Then look for any differences.

```
┌─────────────────┐   Events that bring   ┌─────────────────┐
│ Setting at the  │ → about change     →  │ Setting at the  │
│ beginning of a  │                       │ end of a story  │
│ story           │                       │                 │
└─────────────────┘                       └─────────────────┘
```

Read the selection below. Then answer the question that follows.

Visiting the Library

1   Wednesday is Library Day at Ricardo's school. After lunch, the class visits the library to check out books.

2   Ricardo and his friends sat at their lunch table. The lunchroom was hot and noisy. All the students were yelling. The tables were covered with trays and milk cartons.

3   Ricardo and his classmates walked to the library. The library was cool and quiet. The books were set carefully on the shelves. All the students whispered.

4   Ricardo thought to himself, "I like the library better than the lunchroom."

1 What is the difference between the cafeteria and the library?

A The cafeteria is cool and the library is hot.

B The library is quiet and the cafeteria is loud.

C The cafeteria is organized and the library is messy.

D The library is colorful and the cafeteria is plain.

OCCT PASS 3.2.c. Demonstrate knowledge of setting

Name _____ Date _____

Independent Practice

Read the selection below. Then answer the questions that follow.

The Time Machine

1. Maya was chosen to be the first student to use a new invention. It was a time machine, invented in the year 2050!

2. Maya flew in her car to the laboratory where the time machine was held. In the car, she looked around at her city. The air was filled with smog. The buildings rose high above the clouds. Cars zoomed past her in the air. She saw many trees and birds.

3. Maya had chosen to travel to ancient Egypt.

4. She stepped into the time machine. Instantly she was in some kind of village. The air was clear and the sun was bright. The houses and buildings were low to the ground. There were many trees and birds in the square. Maya noticed her skin felt hot.

5. Suddenly, she was back in her own time. The scientist said, "I'm sorry we had to bring you back so quickly."

6. "That's okay," Maya said. "I like my own time better."

2 Which is one of the settings in the story?

A school
B village hut
C skyscraper
D ancient Egypt

3 How are the two settings similar?

A Both are hot.
B Both have clean air.
C Both have time machines.
D Both have birds and trees.

4 How are the two settings different?

A One is hot, the other is cool.
B One has birds, the other doesn't.
C One has tall buildings, the other has small huts.
D One is a fantasy, the other is a real place.

LESSON 14 Cause and Effect

Cause and effect show how one action leads to another. The first action is the **cause** and the action that follows is the **effect**. Stories and other reading passages often show you how one thing leads to another. Keep track of how causes lead to effects to help you understand what you read.

Read the selection below. Then answer the question that follows.

Inventing an Alphabet

1   Could you invent an alphabet by yourself? In 1809, a man named Sequoyah did. He was a member of the Cherokee tribe.

2   The Cherokee had no way of writing down their ideas or speech. Sequoyah decided to give his people a written language. He used letters to stand for sounds in their spoken language. He could then join the letters to make words.

3   Many Cherokee thought that Sequoyah's idea was silly. However, when he had made his alphabet, he taught it to young people. As a result, they were able to learn to read and write it easily. Sequoyah became a hero.

---

1 What was the effect of Sequoyah teaching the alphabet to the young Cherokee?

- (A) They learned to read and write.
- B They invented their own alphabet.
- C They thought Sequoyah was silly.
- D They made him a member of their tribe.

OCCT PASS 3.4.d. Identify cause/effect relationships in text

Name _____ Date _____

Independent Practice

Read the selection below. Then answer the questions that follow.

The Germ Theory of Disease

1. In the 1800s, a man named Louis Pasteur helped create the germ theory of disease. This theory explained how people become sick. Pasteur's theory said that air is filled with germs. Germs are tiny living things. They cause colds, flu, and many diseases.

2. Pasteur also showed that germs do not just appear. They grow. For example, if you put a few germs in a cup of soup and then kept the cup covered, new germs would grow.

3. The important effect of Pasteur's theory is how milk was treated. Before Pasteur, when people drank milk, germs living in the milk would enter people's bodies and sometimes made them sick.

4. Because of Pasteur's ideas, it became common to heat milk before drinking it. Heating the milk killed the germs inside it. This process was known as *pasteurization*. It was named after Louis Pasteur. Milk is still pasteurized today.

2

What is the effect of heating milk before drinking it?

A It improves the taste of the milk.
B It reduces the fat in the milk.
C It is how people test milk for quality.
D It kills the germs in the milk.

3

What causes people to become sick?

A milk
B soup
C germs
D pasteurization

4

Why did Pasteur study germs?

A Germs were everywhere.
B Germs often made people sick.
C Pasteur made people sick.
D Pasteur treated milk everywhere.

OCCT Test Preparation — Lesson 14

LESSON 15: Biography

Today you will write a biography. A true story about a real person's life is called a **biography**. Biographies are often written about famous people. There are many biographies about actors, athletes, and politicians. Biographies have basic facts, such as where a person was born.

Your writing will be scored on how fully you develop the topic and on how well you organize and express your ideas. Your composition will be scored by trained readers. As you work, keep in mind these three stages of the writing process:

- **Planning:** Take time to plan your writing by listing, outlining, or organizing your ideas in the space provided.

- **Writing:** Write about the topic in a clear and logical manner in the space provided. Make sure your composition is as complete as possible. Be sure to include a beginning, middle, and an ending for your composition.

- **Editing/Revising:** Take time to reread what you have written, and decide if you need to add more details or change the organization of your composition. At the same time, look for and correct any errors in grammar, punctuation, capitalization, and spelling. You may use the *Writer's Checklist* on page 8 of this book to help you revise your writing.

> Look up encyclopedia entries for a U.S. president and write a short biography of him. What did he do as a president? What did he do before that? What is he most remembered for?

OCCT *PASS* Writing 2.4. Write informational pieces with multiple paragraphs

Name _____ Date _____

Independent Practice

Read the prompt below. Then complete the outline and write a biography.

Write about a family member you know well. What has he or she done?

Outline

I. Introduction
-
-

II. Body
-
-
-

III. Conclusion
-
-

_____
_____
_____
_____
_____
_____
_____
_____
_____
_____

LESSON 16: Multiple-Meaning Words and Idioms

Test Preparation

Multiple-meaning words are words that have different meanings depending on the way they are used in a sentence. To figure out the meaning of a word, ask yourself if it is a noun or a verb, and in what context it is used.

Most people keep their money in a *bank*.

I stood on the *bank* of the river, waiting for the boat.

Sometimes a passage can contain expressions that do not mean exactly what they say. Those expressions are called **idioms**.

Nobody was talking, so I decided to *break the ice* and introduce myself.

The idiom *break the ice* means "to start to talk with someone new."

Read the selection below. Then answer the question that follows.

1   When you use good manners, you are polite and show respect for other people.

2   People think that other people who don't use good manners are rude. But they may not know that they are doing anything wrong.

3   If you want to use good manners, here is a tip: start by always saying "please" and "thank you." You may be surprised by people's reactions.

1

In which of these sentences does the word tip have the same meaning as in the article?

A   The waiter received a large tip for his good work.

B   Laura asked me for a tip on where to go on vacation.

C   Jane didn't want to tip over the glass of milk.

D   There was a crumb on the tip of her nose.

OCCT *PASS* 1.3. Apply knowledge of fourth grade level multiple-meaning words and idioms to determine the meanings of words and phrases

Independent Practice

Read the selection below. Then answer the questions that follow.

Fun Art Activities

1   Have you ever felt bored on a rainy day? From now on, you can chase away boredom with art!

2   DRAWING: The easiest way to make art is by drawing. You can draw pictures of things found in nature. Practice drawing pictures of leaves from different kinds of trees.

3   PAINTING: Painting is a little more complicated than drawing. Watercolors are the easiest paints to use. Tempera paints make brighter colors, but they will stain your clothes!

4   SCULPTING: Suppose that you don't want all your art to be flat. Use modeling clay to sculpt figures. Modeling tools help you shape it the way you want it. You could create a whole new zoo of fantastic animals!

5   Finally, if you think you are all thumbs, then pick up a book and read!

2 In which of these sentences does the word underlined draw have the same meaning as in the article?

A   He tried to draw the curtains but they fell on the floor.
B   Karla knows how to draw beautiful landscapes.
C   Albert always wants to draw people's attention.
D   Danny was asked to draw a ticket from the jar.

3 In which of these sentences does the word figures have the same meaning as in the article?

A   He figures that it will be a long night.
B   Sam added up all the figures and got the same result.
C   Public figures are often recognized in the street.
D   The wax figures showed what dinosaurs looked like.

4 What does the idiom "all thumbs" mean?

A   clumsy
B   excited
C   crafty
D   bored

LESSON 17 Organization

Organization is how ideas are linked together in a piece of writing. In expository and informational text, authors use headings and subheadings to introduce ideas. Headings are often larger and bolder than subheadings. Expository text also includes a clear introduction, body, and conclusion.

To figure out how a selection is organized, look for headings and subheadings. Think of the heading as the main idea and the subheadings as the details that tell more about, or give examples of, the main idea.

GREAT DOGS OF THE WORLD — Heading and Main Idea of Selection

Dog Breeds — Subheading and Supporting Detail of Selection

Read the selection below. Then answer the question that follows.

Spanish Languages

1. **What Is an Accent?**
If you are from Oklahoma, you might find it hard to understand someone from Scotland. Although both of you speak English, it's the accent, or way of speaking each word, that makes it hard to understand.

2. **How Is Language Different?**
Language has its own words and rules. People who speak different languages often can't understand each other.

3. **Language Regions of Spain**
In Spain, different regions, also speak different languages. The official language of Spain is *Castilian*. However, Spain is home to three other languages: *Catalan*, *Galician*, and *Basque*.

---

1 Which of these headings is the main idea of the selection?

A Spanish Languages
B How Is Language Different?
C What Is an Accent?
D Language Regions of Spain

OCCT *PASS* 5.1.a. Understand the organization of and access information from a variety of sources

Name Elijah #12   Date _____

Independent Practice

Read the selection below. Then answer the questions that follow.

Recipe for the World's Best Mashed Potatoes

1   Here's a recipe guaranteed to make the world's best mashed potatoes.

2   **You Will Need:**
1 lb of potatoes, peeled and halved
$\frac{1}{2}$ tsp of salt
2 tbsp of butter
1 tbsp of milk
Salt and pepper
Potato masher

3   **Directions:**
- Place potatoes and salt into a large saucepan and fill with water.
- Boil the water. Then reduce heat to a simmer.
- Simmer the potatoes for 15–20 minutes, or until soft.
- Warm butter in the microwave until it melts.
- Strain water from the cooked potatoes and place them in a bowl.
- Add melted butter to bowl.
- Mash the potatoes with a potato masher until broken up.
- Add milk until your mashed potatoes are creamy.
- Add salt and pepper to taste.

2 How is paragraph 3 organized?
- A sequential order
- B alphabetical order
- C numerical order
- D chronological order

3 How is paragraph 2 organized?
- A from largest amount to smallest amount
- B the order in which the author buys the ingredients
- C from the most to the least tasty
- D the order in which ingredients are used

4 Which item is a supporting detail in the selection?
- A Here's a recipe guaranteed to make the world's best mashed potatoes.
- B You Will Need
- C Recipe for the World's Best Mashed Potatoes
- D Add salt and pepper to taste.

OCCT Test Preparation   Lesson 17

LESSON 18 Chronological Order

Sometimes you will need to determine the order of events in a story or an article. In a story, this is called **chronological order**. Another name for chronological order is *sequence*. When you are reading, you should pay close attention to the order in which things happen. Ask yourself what happened *first* in a passage and what happened *last*. Keep track of how one thing leads to another. Remembering the order in which things happen will help you understand what you are reading.

Transition and signal words can help you keep track of the order of events. Words such as *first, second, last, before, after,* and *then* are clues that tell you about the chronological order and sequence.

Read the selection below. Then answer the question that follows.

How Peanut Butter Is Made

1. Have you ever wondered how peanut butter is made? Peanut butter begins with the farmers who grow the peanuts. Peanut farmers use special machines for planting and harvesting.

2. After the harvest, farmers bring the peanuts to a plant where the shells are removed. The unshelled peanuts are then shipped to the peanut butter factory.

3. At the peanut butter factory, the nuts are checked for quality and then roasted in special ovens. The roasted peanuts go through a machine that rubs off the skins.

4. Next, the peanuts are ground until they turn into a smooth cream. Finally, the fresh peanut butter is put into a jar and shipped to the stores to be sold.

---

1 What happens <u>before</u> the peanuts are shipped to the peanut butter factory?

A The peanuts have their skins removed.
B The peanuts are roasted in ovens.
C The peanut butter is put into a jar.
D The peanut shells are removed.

OCCT *PASS* 3.4.d. Analyze and explain sequences from a text

Name _____   Date _____

Independent Practice

Read the selection below. Then answer the questions that follow.

How to Build a Birdhouse

1. Follow these steps to make a simple birdhouse. Be sure to have an adult help you.
2. **You Will Need:**
   - milk carton
   - stapler
   - masking tape
   - brown shoe polish
   - safety scissors
   - ruler
   - pencil
   - heavy-duty string
3. Wash and rinse an empty half-gallon milk carton.
4. Next, close the carton and staple it shut.
5. Then, cover the surface of the carton with small strips of masking tape.
6. Use brown shoe polish. This will make the birdhouse look as though it was made of bark.
7. Then, use safety scissors to cut a hole in the side of the milk carton. The hole should be about 2 inches across and about 6 inches from the bottom of the carton. Check your measurements with a ruler.
8. Use a pencil to punch holes in the bottom and top of the carton. The bottom holes will let rain drain out of the birdhouse. The top holes will let air in.
9. Finally, punch a small hole at the top of your birdhouse. Thread the string through the hole and tie it into a loop. Then hang the birdhouse from a small tree branch.

2 What is the last step in building the birdhouse?

A poking holes in the top and bottom of the carton

B using shoe polish to color the tape

C stapling the top of the carton shut

D hanging the birdhouse on a tree branch

3 What should you do after cutting a hole in the side of the carton but before making a loop of string?

A Wash the milk carton and rinse it thoroughly.

B Find a small tree branch for the birdhouse.

C Put holes in the top and bottom of the house with a pencil.

D Put a layer of tape on the carton.

OCCT Test Preparation   Lesson 18

LESSON 19 Punctuation and Capitalization

You use **punctuation** and **capitalization** as signposts to help you understand what you read. Without correct punctuation and capitalization, a piece of writing would be very difficult to read. Look at the chart below for some capitalization and punctuation rules.

Read the selection below. Then answer the question that follows.

Punctuation	Example
End punctuation	We are going to the beach. Would you like to come? I love swimming!
Commas	After I went home, I ate lunch. I ate salad, bread, and cheese.
Quotation marks	"I like this weather," she said. "It is warm but not humid."
Apostrophes	Please don't tease your brother. That is your sister's toy.

Capitalization	Example
Names and titles	**J**ulia **R**odriguez **M**ayor **W**illiams
Holidays	**T**hanksgiving **D**ay **I**ndependence **D**ay
Product names	**F**untime **V**ideos **T**oybot **G**ames
Locations	**A**ustralia **S**outh **B**end, **I**ndiana

1. In which sentence below is all punctuation correct?

A Is the cat enjoying her toy.
B Is the cat enjoying her toy!
C Is the cat enjoying her toy?
D Is the cat, enjoying her toy?

OCCT *PASS* 2.1. Read and comprehend

Name _____ Date _____

Independent Practice

Answer the questions that follow.

2

Which book title is capitalized correctly?

A a Tale of Two Cities
B a Tale Of Two Cities
C A Tale Of Two Cities
D A Tale of Two Cities

3

In which sentence below is **all** punctuation correct?

A We have English math, and social studies every morning.
B We have English, math and social studies every morning.
C We have English, math, and social studies every morning.
D We have English math, and social studie's every morning.

4

In which sentence below is **all** punctuation correct?

A Did you bring your book the teacher asked.
B "Did you bring your book?" the teacher asked.
C "Did you bring your book," the teacher asked.
D "Did you bring your book!" the teacher asked?

5

In which sentence below is **all** capitalization correct?

A dad said, "We will take a trip to Alexandria, Virginia, next summer."
B Dad said, "We will take a trip to alexandria, Virginia, next Summer."
C Dad said, "we will take a trip to Alexandria, Virginia, next Summer."
D Dad said, "We will take a trip to Alexandria, Virginia, next summer."

6

In which sentence below is **all** capitalization correct?

A Every Wednesday, Ms. davison takes our class to the School library.
B Every Wednesday, ms. Davison takes our class to the school library.
C Every Wednesday, Ms. Davison takes our class to the school library.
D Every wednesday, Ms. Davison takes our class to the School Library.

OCCT Test Preparation

LESSON 20 Creative Narrative

Today you will write a **narrative** on an assigned topic. Last time, your narrative was nonfiction. This time, the prompt requires a creative response.

Your writing will be scored on how fully you develop the topic and on how well you organize and express your ideas. Your composition will be scored by trained readers. As you work, keep in mind these three stages of the writing process:

- **Planning:** Take time to plan your writing by listing, outlining, or organizing your ideas in the space provided.

- **Writing:** Write about the topic in a clear and logical manner in the space provided. Make sure your composition is as complete as possible. Be sure to include a beginning, middle, and an ending for your composition.

- **Editing/Revising:** Take time to reread what you have written, and decide if you need to add more details or change the organization of your composition. At the same time, look for and correct any errors in grammar, punctuation, capitalization, and spelling. You may use the *Writer's Checklist* on page 8 of this book to help you revise your writing.

Write a science fiction story about a kid your age living on another planet. Be sure to include multiple characters, dialogue, and descriptions of setting. Try to use vivid verbs and adjectives. Use your imagination!

OCCT *PASS* Writing 2.1. Write narrative compositions

Name _____ Date _____

Independent Practice

Read the prompt below. Then complete the organizer and write a narrative.

Write a story that takes place in the Wild West. Include many characters and describe the setting. Your story can be realistic, but it must be fiction.

Story Components

Character	Setting	Plot

_____
_____
_____
_____
_____
_____
_____
_____
_____
_____
_____
_____
_____
_____

LESSON 21: Author's Purpose

Authors write for different purposes, or reasons. In most nonfiction, the **author's purpose** is to inform or explain. Some nonfiction authors write to persuade. Fiction authors usually write to entertain.

Sometimes an author states his or her purpose. Often, you must discover the author's purpose from the text.

Author's Purpose	Description	Example of Text
To inform or explain	• nonfiction • presents facts	Lincoln was born in a log cabin with a dirt floor.
To persuade	• tells what to do or think	It is every citizen's duty to vote. Be sure to do your duty.
To entertain	• usually fiction • has characters and events	Judy could see the clouds darkening. She knew that she had to get down the mountain.

Read the selection below. Then answer the question that follows.

1   Clayton glanced quickly at the scoreboard as he dribbled down the court. The score was 55-52, with just a little more than one minute left.

2   Clayton knew that his team couldn't lose the ball now, and it couldn't miss this next basket. If his team missed, the Manatees would lose the league title, and the season would be over.

3   With his heart racing, Clayton bounce-passed to Derek. Derek turned, shot the ball, and scored!

1 What was the author's purpose in writing this story?

A   to inform readers about basketball

B   to tell an exciting story about basketball

C   to persuade readers to watch basketball games

D   to explain what basketball players think about

OCCT PASS 4.2.b. Identify the purposes of different types of texts

Name _____ Date _____

Independent Practice

Read the selection below. Then answer the questions that follow.

Let's Change the Playground Now!

1 We are proud of Dalton School. We have so many terrific teachers and good students. Mr. Stein is a hardworking, caring principal. However, one thing we are not proud of is the playground. We have studied the use of the playground at recess for one year. As a result, we know that the playground has several pieces of dangerous equipment.

2 The jungle gym is dangerous and should be removed. Several children have hurt themselves going through the tunnel part of the structure. One child was injured in a fall from the high bars. In one place, the wood is uneven and causes many falls. The jungle gym should be replaced as soon as possible. We also need a new slide. It should be wider. It needs better, safer stairs. It should probably be moved to a new location so that the landing area is farther away from the basketball court. Finally, we need better swings. All the chains are rusted, and many of the swings have broken seats.

3 As members of the Dalton School Parent Association, we care about Dalton School. We hope that these changes to the playground can be made as soon as possible.

2 What was the author's purpose in writing "Let's Change the Playground Now!"?

A to describe the jungle gym, swings, and slide

B to explain the purpose of the Dalton School Parent Association

C to persuade readers to make the school playground safe

D to tell stories about accidents on the playground and at school

3 What was the author's purpose in including paragraph 2?

A to explain what is wrong with each piece of equipment

B to tell a story about children on the playground

C to tell what people at the school have done wrong

D to inform people about the cost of playground improvement

LESSON 22 Compare and Contrast

A **comparison** shows how characters, places, and events are alike. One way to find a comparison is to look for the word *like*. Then decide what is being compared.

Comparison	What Is Compared	Why They Are Compared
The clouds were *like* pillows.	clouds and pillows	to show that the clouds looked comfortable or soft enough to lie on

A **contrast** shows how characters, places, and events are different.

One common type of contrast shows how people, characters, and things change over time.

Contrast	What Is Contrasted	Why They Are Contrasted
Before the game, Sarah could not sit still. She stretched her arms and legs. She ran in place along the sidelines. When the game was over, Sarah fell in an exhausted heap. She did not have a drop of energy left.	Sarah's feelings before and after the game	to show that Sarah is excited and full of energy before the game but exhausted after the game.

Read the selection below. Then answer the question that follows.

1   Jonathan had never been on stage in front of the whole school before. Did everyone know how nervous he was? He was sure that his face was red, and his heart was pounding. His biggest problem was that his whole body was trembling.

2   Would the audience notice that his hands were like flags in a strong wind? Everyone told Jonathan that he would be fine once he got on stage, but that was hard for him to believe right now.

1

Jonathan's hands are compared to "flags in a strong wind" because both are

A small.
B on stage.
C flapping.
D problems.

OCCT *PASS* 4.4. Compare and contrast characters

Lesson 22   Page 51   OCCT Test Preparation

Independent Practice

Read the selection below. Then answer the questions that follow.

A Gift for Mom

1   Mother's Day was only two days away, and Meredith was worried. Her brother, Ethan, had bought their mom a bar of soap that smelled like lilacs. Her sister, Gillian, had bought a magazine about fishing, her mom's favorite hobby. Meredith felt bad because she didn't have a gift. She sighed and decided to make a card.

2   As Meredith wrote her card, she thought of all the things that her mother had done for her in just the past few days. She began to make a list. She listed everything, from help with homework to rides to soccer practice. She even listed kisses and hugs. When she was finished, she copied her list in her best writing on light blue paper. She drew a border of pink hearts.

3   When her mother opened Ethan's present on Mother's Day, she hugged Ethan and told him how much she liked lilac soap. When she opened Gillian's present, she exclaimed, "Just what I wanted!" and hugged Gillian. When she read Meredith's list, though, her eyes looked like <u>small ponds</u>, and then the tears fell. "Oh, Meredith!" she sobbed. "I love this!" Meredith knew hers was the best gift of all.

2 Which sentence best compares and contrasts Meredith's feelings about her gift during the story?

A At first she wanted to give her mother soap, but later she made a card.

B At first she was excited about her gift, but later she thought it was bad.

C At first she wanted to buy a gift, but later she wanted to draw a picture.

D At first she worried about her gift, but later she knew her gift was special.

3 Meredith's mother's eyes are compared to "small ponds" because they are

A both wet.

B not deep.

C both shiny.

D not small.

LESSON 23 Context Clues

Often when you are reading, you will come across words you do not know. You could use a dictionary to look up their meanings. You can also try to figure out the meanings of the words using context clues. **Context clues** are hints in a passage that make understanding difficult words easier. If you understand the rest of the passage, you may be able to figure out what the words mean.

Read the selection below. Then answer the questions that follow.

Where's the Mail?

Lunchtime came and went, but no mail showed up. That was strange. Usually the mail carrier came every afternoon around 12:30. By four o'clock, Kendra wondered whether something was different about today. The mail never <u>arrived</u> this late. Suddenly, she <u>realized</u> what was happening. Today was Memorial Day! Her package would have to wait another day.

---

1 In this passage, what does <u>arrived</u> mean?

A left
B came
C slept
D sorted

2 Kendra remembered it was Memorial Day. Therefore, we can infer that <u>realize</u> means to

A understand clearly.
B persuade fully.
C describe completely.
D inform quickly.

OCCT *PASS* 2.2. Read challenging texts

Name _____ Date _____

Independent Practice

Read the selection below. Then answer the questions that follow.

The Snowman

1. It had snowed for the first time. Sam and Carla <u>elected</u> to build a snowman. They made three balls of snow and stacked them to make the snowman's body. Then it was time to make the face. They <u>affixed</u> small berries in the shape of a smile and used a carrot for a nose.

2. "I think it's supposed to have coal for eyes," said Sam.

3. "Where do we get coal?" asked Carla.

4. Sam had no answer for that. Instead of coal, the two stuck an old pair of sunglasses on the snowman. Everyone <u>concurred</u>: Sam and Carla's snowman was the best one in town.

3 What does <u>elected</u> mean?
- A decided
- B voted
- C realized
- D declined

4 Which word has almost the <u>same</u> meaning as <u>affixed</u>?
- A ate
- B found
- C planted
- D attached

5 What does <u>concurred</u> mean?
- A took over
- B denied
- C agreed
- D dreamed

LESSON 24: Reference Information

In order to better understand an article, you might need to use **reference information** such as charts, illustrations, and diagrams. Each type of reference information shows information in different ways. Always begin by reading the title of the chart, map, or diagram.

Charts are graphic organizers that compare information by showing it in rows and columns. Columns run from top to bottom on a chart. Rows run across a chart from left to right. The kinds of information are listed in the headings. Headings appear at the top of each column and often at the beginning of each row. Read all the headings after you have read the title.

Diagrams are labeled drawings that show the parts of something or show how something works. **Illustrations** show information in pictures. On charts and diagrams, read numbered labels in order.

Read the selection below. Then answer the question that follows.

Types of Fats You Eat

Type of Fat	Where You Find It	Advice for Good Health
Unsaturated fats	olive and peanut oils, nuts, avocados	Eat these fats in small amounts each day.
Saturated fats	butter, cheese, meat, ice cream, whole milk	You can sometimes eat small amounts of these fats.
Trans fats	margarine, many packaged baked goods, most fast food	Try to avoid eating these fats.

1 Based on this chart, which type of food is best to eat?

A butter
B margarine
C meat
D nuts

OCCT *PASS* 5.1.a. Understand the organization of and access information from a variety of sources

Name _____   Date _____

Independent Practice

Read the selection below. Then answer the questions that follow.

Metric Measures of Length

Unit of Measure	Equal to	Approximately the Same Length as
1 centimeter	10 millimeters	the width of your fingertip
1 decimeter	10 centimeters	the height of a yogurt container
1 meter	100 centimeters	the distance from the floor to a doorknob
1 kilometer	1,000 meters	the distance around two city blocks

2 Based on the chart, which is the best unit of measure for measuring your own height?

A centimeter
B decimeter
C meter
D kilometer

4 Which of the following lengths is most likely measured in centimeters?

A the legs of a flea
B the wings of an airplane
C the depth of an ocean
D the width of a sheet of paper

3 Based on the chart, a meter is

A longer than a centimeter but shorter than a decimeter.
B shorter than a decimeter but longer than a kilometer.
C longer than a decimeter but shorter than a kilometer.
D shorter than both a kilometer and a decimeter.

OCCT Test Preparation   Page 56   Lesson 24

LESSON 25 Research

Good writers need to be able to research their subjects before writing. **Research** is the process of collecting information on a subject. Fiction authors research the settings of their stories. Nonfiction authors research the facts about their subjects.

When you do research, you have to use good sources. Good sources include published books, encyclopedias, videos, and trusted Internet sites. In this lesson, you will do research and then write a report on your findings.

When you take the OCCT, your writing will be scored on how fully you develop the topic and on how well you organize and express your ideas. Your composition will be scored by trained readers. As you work, keep in mind these three stages of the writing process:

- **Planning:** Take time to plan your writing by listing, outlining, or organizing your ideas in the space provided.

- **Writing:** Write about the topic in a clear and logical manner in the space provided. Make sure your composition is as complete as possible. Be sure to include a beginning, middle, and an ending for your composition.

- **Editing/Revising:** Take time to reread what you have written, and decide if you need to add more details or change the organization of your composition. At the same time, look for and correct any errors in grammar, punctuation, capitalization, and spelling. You may use the *Writer's Checklist* on page 8 of this book to help you revise your writing.

> **Research an endangered species using two sources. One source should be online, and the other should be a published book other than an encyclopedia. In your report, summarize what you learned.**

OCCT *PASS* Writing 2.4. Write informational pieces with multiple paragraphs

Name _____ Date _____

Independent Practice

Read the writing prompt below. Then complete the graphic organizer and write a composition.

Research an important woman in history. Try to use more than one source. In your report, summarize what you learned. Use vivid language to describe your subject.

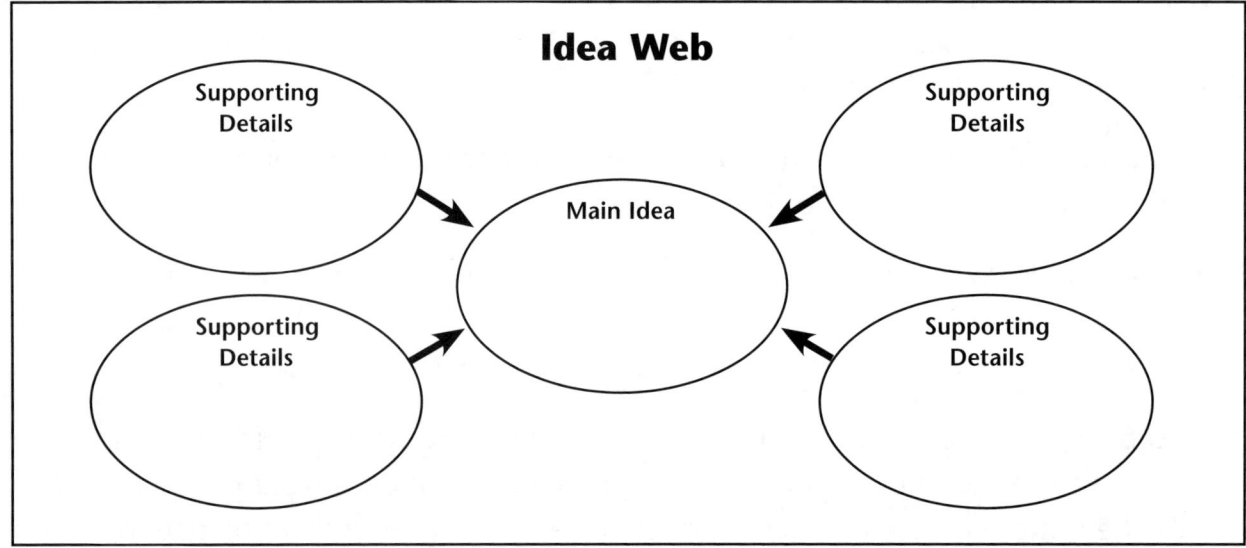

LESSON 26 Conflict and Conflict Resolution

The plot of a story is often based on a conflict. **Conflict** is the main problem in a story. **Conflict resolution** is how the characters in the story solve their problem.

To find the conflict, ask these questions:
- Does anyone in the story face a problem?
- What is the problem?
- How is the problem fixed or resolved?

The conflict resolution is usually at the end of the story.

Read the selection below. Then answer the question that follows.

The Party

1   It was just four days until the party when Willa began to suspect that something was going on.

2   Katie and Tamara were always whispering to each other. Sometimes they even looked Willa's way. Sometimes they snickered.

3   Willa asked Katie what she and Tamara were up to and why they were always telling secrets.

3   When Katie shrugged off the question, Willa became angry.

4   "You're supposed to be my friend!" she shouted. "But you won't even answer me."

5   All that greeted Willa was Katie's blank stare. She stomped off in a huff, determined to find some new friends.

6   It wasn't until days later that Willa learned of the surprise party Katie and Tamara had planned for her.

1

What is Willa's <u>biggest</u> conflict in the story?

A   Katie is angry at Tamara.
B   Katie is friends with Tamara.
C   Her friend Katie tells secrets.
D   Tamara wants to be Katie's friend.

OCCT PASS 4.2.a. Identify the main events of the plot

Independent Practice

Read the selection below. Then answer the questions that follow.

Saturday

1 It was a perfect Saturday afternoon. Tomás was about to join Jamey and some of the other kids who were playing soccer at Dan's house. Just then, Mr. Ramirez said to Tomás, "Let's go to the Science Museum!"

2 "No way!" thought Tomás, who just wanted to be with his friends. He thought museums were boring places where grownups got excited about things that kids didn't understand. Still, he knew that when his dad got an idea, it was hard to say, "No."

3 At first, Tomás shuffled through the museum, irritating his dad. But then they went to the wild animal show. The featured animal was a parrot. When Tomás was chosen as the audience volunteer who got to come on stage and hold the parrot, he got a big shock. It was a little scary at first, but Tomás also felt special and proud. At one point, the parrot perched on his shoulder. Everyone laughed and clapped.

4 When he left the stage, the audience cheered again. He sat down and asked, "Dad, what animal are they featuring next Saturday?" Tomás couldn't wait to go home and tell Jamey, Dan, and the other kids all about it.

---

2 What is the conflict in this story?

A Tomás is irritating his father.

B Tomás doesn't want to go to the museum.

C Dan does not want Tomás to play soccer.

D Mr. Ramirez wants Tomás to get a pet parrot.

3 What is the conflict resolution in this story?

A Mr. Ramirez buys a parrot.

B Dan lets Tomás play soccer.

C Tomás enjoys his time at the museum.

D Tomás decides not to go to the museum.

LESSON 27: Fact and Opinion

Information that is known to be true is a **fact**. You can also prove a fact to be true. Other writing includes opinion. An **opinion** is someone's point of view. When reading, it is important that you understand the difference between fact and opinion so that you will know whether you are reading a true statement or someone's thoughts.

Read the selection below. Then answer the question that follows.

1   Dear Helen,

2   It is May, which is a beautiful time in Saint Petersburg. Saint Petersburg is the second largest city in Russia. Saint Petersburg is special because it is very close to the North Pole. That means that during the summer it is light all night. At the end of June we have a big celebration.

3   Saint Petersburg is built on more than one hundred islands. That means we have hundreds of bridges. The Blue Bridge is almost 100 meters wide. That's about 330 feet. The biggest river here is called the Neva. Saint Petersburg has a lot of impressive buildings, such as churches, fortresses, and museums. Some people say that Saint Petersburg is the most interesting city in Russia.

4   The city is also a fun place to be. There is a lot to do here. And the people are very nice. If you ever come to Russia, you should visit Saint Petersburg.

5   Your pen pal,
    Sergei

1

Which sentence from the selection is an opinion?

A The biggest river here is called the Neva.

B The Blue Bridge is almost 100 meters wide.

C At the end of June we have a big celebration.

D Saint Petersburg is the most interesting city in Russia.

OCCT *PASS* 3.4.c. Identify fact and opinion

Name _____ Date _____

Independent Practice

Read the selection below. Then answer the questions that follow.

Come to Antarctica!

1   Have you ever really wanted to get away from it all? Come and check out Antarctica! Take a cruise and visit the world's coldest place!

2   Antarctica is gorgeous. It is full of tall, snowy peaks. The blue glaciers are nothing short of breathtaking.

3   You'll also see lots of animals you can't find anywhere else. There are many kinds of penguins, seals, and whales. Have a look at the snow petrel—a bird that bathes in snow!

4   While you're here, we'll host you in our famous Edge of the World Hotel. The food is delicious, and the heaters run twenty-four hours a day.

For more information, contact Travel Tours at 1-888-9578 today!

2 This advertisement includes

A only facts.
B both facts and opinions.
C only opinions.
D neither facts nor opinions.

3 Which is a fact?

A The blue glaciers are nothing short of breathtaking.
B The food is delicious.
C Antarctica is home to animals that don't live anywhere else.
D Antarctica is gorgeous.

4 Which is an opinion?

A The food is delicious.
B Have a look at the snow petrel—a bird that bathes in snow!
C The heaters run twenty-four hours a day.
D You'll also see lots of animals you can't find anywhere else.

OCCT Test Preparation • Lesson 27

LESSON 28: Similarities and Differences in Characters

When characters are **similar** to each other, they are alike. When characters are **different** from each other, they are unalike. When you read a story, you may think about ways in which characters are similar or different. To find similarities and differences, think about what characters do, say, and think.

Characters can change during the story. Think about how the character is at the beginning of the story and then at the end of the story. Then look for any differences.

Character at the beginning of a story → Events that bring about change → Character at the end of a story

Read the selection below. Then answer the question that follows.

1 Hanna's stomach was tied up in knots. She was nervous because today's test was an important part of her grade.

2 But Hanna knew what to do—she went to her friend, Jamal. Jamal was a great math student.

3 Hanna asked Jamal, "Will you tutor me before the math test today?"

4 "Yes, I will tutor you, Hanna. We will work together," said Jamal.

5 "Thanks, Jamal," said Hanna. Hanna felt a lot less nervous!

1. Which is a <u>difference</u> between Jamal and Hanna?

A Jamal is a good tutor, but Hanna is not.

B Hanna is a good friend, but Jamal is not.

C Jamal is bad at math, but Hanna is good at math.

D Hanna gets nervous before tests, but Jamal is calm.

OCCT *PASS* 3.2.c. Identify characters' qualities

Name _____ Date _____

Independent Practice

Read the selection below. Then answer the questions that follow.

Michael Goes to Bat

1   Michael had been keeping the bench warm for three innings, which wasn't that unusual for him. When the team was far ahead or far behind, Coach Walters always put Michael in the game. But when the game was close, as it was today, Michael usually sat it out. Whenever this happened, he tried to keep his head up, but it got to him sometimes.

2   Today, Michael was surprised when Coach Walters told him that he would be up in the fourth inning. Michael was following LuAnn Dobbs, a solid base hitter. As he practiced swinging, Michael told himself that he could get a hit. The truth was, though, that Michael had not had a hit all season.

3   When Michael stepped up to the plate, he focused on LuAnn on second base. Then, as he heard his mom yell out, "Go, Michael! Go Reds!" he gathered up his strength. On the very first pitch, he heard the sweet, solid sound of the bat connecting with the ball. It was no home run, but Michael made it safely to first base as LuAnn, a speedy runner, crossed home plate to tie the game.

4   Michael and LuAnn both cheered! They were both happy their team was winning.

2

How does Michael change in the story?

A At first he is warming the bench. Then he gets his first hit of the season.

B At first he feels bad about the coach. Then he feels better about the coach.

C At first he does not think he will get a hit. Then he knows that he can do it.

D At first he will not hit the ball. Then he knows he will win the game for his team.

3

How are Michael and LuAnn different?

A LuAnn is a slower runner than Michael is.

B LuAnn likes the coach more than Michael does.

C LuAnn gets a hit more often than Michael does.

D Michael believes in himself more than LuAnn believes in herself.

LESSON 29 Cause and Effect

Cause and effect show how one action leads to another. The first action is the **cause** and the action that follows is the **effect**. Stories and other reading passages often show you how one thing leads to another. Keep track of how causes lead to effects to help you understand what you read.

To find causes and effects when reading, look for these clue words: *because, if, then, since, therefore, so that, as a result,* and *when*. Causes, effects, and clue words can appear anywhere in a sentence.

Cause	Clue Word	Effect
Lauren and I were tired.	*Therefore,*	we went to bed.

Effect	Clue Word	Cause
James was feeling lonely	*because*	his friends were not around.

Clue Word	Cause	Effect
As a result	*of the bad weather,*	the game was canceled.

Read the selection below. Then answer the question that follows.

Hiding in the House

1 Because it's a surprise party,
  We're all hiding in the house.
  So that Priya doesn't know I'm here,
  I'm just as quiet as a mouse.

5 When Priya walks in the door,
  She'll think that we didn't care.
  But when we all jump up and shout,
  Sounds of love will fill the air.

---

1 What effect does Priya walking into the house have?

A Everyone leaves.
B Everyone is quiet.
C Everyone jumps up and shouts.
D Everyone gives her cake and gifts.

OCCT *PASS* 3.4.d. Identify cause and effect relationships in text

Name _____ Date _____

Independent Practice

Read the selection below. Then answer the questions that follow.

Gossip

1 Because Jason was a gossip,
And Linda was all ears,
Soon everyone in the school knew
About Benjamin's worst fears.

5 When Benjamin heard the gossip,
He asked Jason to please tell why
He could have been so heartless
To such an easygoing guy.

As a result of Benjamin's question,
10 Jason turned as shy as a sheep.

He muttered and he stammered,
"I'm sorry I was such a creep."

Next, Benjamin went to Linda
And asked Linda to please tell why
15 She had been so cruel and nasty
To such a friendly, happy guy.

When Linda heard the question
She acted shy and quiet, too.
"I'll never gossip again," she said.
20 "It's a terrible thing to do."

---

2 What causes Benjamin to talk to Jason?

A Benjamin knows that Linda spread the gossip.
B Benjamin heard that Jason was spreading gossip about him.
C Benjamin hears Jason muttering and stammering.
D Benjamin has fears that he does not want anyone to know about.

3 Why does Linda say that she will never gossip again?

A because Benjamin is a friendly, happy guy
B because Jason embarrasses her by asking her about it
C because she knows that it is a terrible thing to do
D because she wants to show Benjamin how much she has changed

---

OCCT Test Preparation   Page 66   Lesson 29

Informational Expository

Informational Expository writing tells readers facts about a topic. Examples of informational expository writing include newspaper and magazine articles, nonfiction books, encyclopedia entries, business reports, academic work, biographies, and other kinds of factual writing. Expository writing has a clear introduction, body, and conclusion.

When you take the OCCT, your writing will be scored on how fully you develop the topic and on how well you organize and express your ideas. Your composition will be scored by trained readers. As you work, keep in mind these three stages of the writing process:

- **Planning:** Take time to plan your writing by listing, outlining, or organizing your ideas in the space provided.

- **Writing:** Write about the topic in a clear and logical manner in the space provided. Make sure your composition is as complete as possible. Be sure to include a beginning, middle, and an ending for your composition.

- **Editing/Revising:** Take time to reread what you have written, and decide if you need to add more details or change the organization of your composition. At the same time, look for and correct any errors in grammar, punctuation, capitalization, and spelling. You may use the *Writer's Checklist* on page 8 of this book to help you revise your writing.

Write about one of your favorite activities. Don't tell about you doing the activity. Instead, give readers facts about the activity. How is it done? Who does it better than anyone else? Try to come up with other details that illustrate the activity.

OCCT *PASS* Writing 2.4. Write informational pieces with multiple paragraphs

Name _____ Date _____

Independent Practice

Read the writing prompt below. Then complete the outline and write an informational expository response.

A fad is something that's popular right now, but soon may not be. What are some fads in your school? Try to come up with other details that illustrate these fads.

Outline

I. Introduction
   A.
   B.
II. Body
   A.
   B.
   C.
III. Conclusion
   A.
   B.

OCCT Test Preparation

Name _____ Date _____

ANSWER DOCUMENT

Lesson 1
Student Practice
1. Ⓐ Ⓑ Ⓒ Ⓓ
2. Ⓐ Ⓑ Ⓒ Ⓓ
3. Ⓐ Ⓑ Ⓒ Ⓓ
4. Ⓐ Ⓑ Ⓒ Ⓓ

Transparency
1. Ⓐ Ⓑ Ⓒ Ⓓ
2. Ⓐ Ⓑ Ⓒ Ⓓ
3. Ⓐ Ⓑ Ⓒ Ⓓ

Lesson 2
Student Practice
1. Ⓐ Ⓑ Ⓒ Ⓓ
2. Ⓐ Ⓑ Ⓒ Ⓓ
3. Ⓐ Ⓑ Ⓒ Ⓓ

Transparency
1. Ⓐ Ⓑ Ⓒ Ⓓ
2. Ⓐ Ⓑ Ⓒ Ⓓ
3. Ⓐ Ⓑ Ⓒ Ⓓ

Lesson 3
Student Practice
1. Ⓐ Ⓑ Ⓒ Ⓓ
2. Ⓐ Ⓑ Ⓒ Ⓓ
3. Ⓐ Ⓑ Ⓒ Ⓓ

Transparency
1. Ⓐ Ⓑ Ⓒ Ⓓ
2. Ⓐ Ⓑ Ⓒ Ⓓ
3. Ⓐ Ⓑ Ⓒ Ⓓ

Lesson 4
Student Practice
1. Ⓐ Ⓑ Ⓒ Ⓓ
2. Ⓐ Ⓑ Ⓒ Ⓓ
3. Ⓐ Ⓑ Ⓒ Ⓓ

Transparency
1. Ⓐ Ⓑ Ⓒ Ⓓ
2. Ⓐ Ⓑ Ⓒ Ⓓ
3. Ⓐ Ⓑ Ⓒ Ⓓ

Lesson 6
Student Practice
1. Ⓐ Ⓑ Ⓒ Ⓓ
2. Ⓐ Ⓑ Ⓒ Ⓓ
3. Ⓐ Ⓑ Ⓒ Ⓓ

Transparency
1. Ⓐ Ⓑ Ⓒ Ⓓ
2. Ⓐ Ⓑ Ⓒ Ⓓ
3. Ⓐ Ⓑ Ⓒ Ⓓ

Lesson 7
Student Practice
1. Ⓐ Ⓑ Ⓒ Ⓓ
2. Ⓐ Ⓑ Ⓒ Ⓓ
3. Ⓐ Ⓑ Ⓒ Ⓓ

Transparency
1. Ⓐ Ⓑ Ⓒ Ⓓ
2. Ⓐ Ⓑ Ⓒ Ⓓ
3. Ⓐ Ⓑ Ⓒ Ⓓ

Lesson 8
Student Practice
1. Ⓐ Ⓑ Ⓒ Ⓓ
2. Ⓐ Ⓑ Ⓒ Ⓓ
3. Ⓐ Ⓑ Ⓒ Ⓓ

Transparency
1. Ⓐ Ⓑ Ⓒ Ⓓ
2. Ⓐ Ⓑ Ⓒ Ⓓ
3. Ⓐ Ⓑ Ⓒ Ⓓ

Lesson 9
Student Practice
1. Ⓐ Ⓑ Ⓒ Ⓓ
2. Ⓐ Ⓑ Ⓒ Ⓓ
3. Ⓐ Ⓑ Ⓒ Ⓓ

Transparency
1. Ⓐ Ⓑ Ⓒ Ⓓ
2. Ⓐ Ⓑ Ⓒ Ⓓ
3. Ⓐ Ⓑ Ⓒ Ⓓ

Lesson 11
Student Practice
1. Ⓐ Ⓑ Ⓒ Ⓓ
2. Ⓐ Ⓑ Ⓒ Ⓓ
3. Ⓐ Ⓑ Ⓒ Ⓓ
4. Ⓐ Ⓑ Ⓒ Ⓓ

Transparency
1. Ⓐ Ⓑ Ⓒ Ⓓ
2. Ⓐ Ⓑ Ⓒ Ⓓ
3. Ⓐ Ⓑ Ⓒ Ⓓ

Lesson 12
Student Practice
1. Ⓐ Ⓑ Ⓒ Ⓓ
2. Ⓐ Ⓑ Ⓒ Ⓓ
3. Ⓐ Ⓑ Ⓒ Ⓓ
4. Ⓐ Ⓑ Ⓒ Ⓓ

Transparency
1. Ⓐ Ⓑ Ⓒ Ⓓ
2. Ⓐ Ⓑ Ⓒ Ⓓ
3. Ⓐ Ⓑ Ⓒ Ⓓ

Name _____ Date _____

Lesson 13
Student Practice
1. Ⓐ Ⓑ Ⓒ Ⓓ
2. Ⓐ Ⓑ Ⓒ Ⓓ
3. Ⓐ Ⓑ Ⓒ Ⓓ
4. Ⓐ Ⓑ Ⓒ Ⓓ

Transparency
1. Ⓐ Ⓑ Ⓒ Ⓓ
2. Ⓐ Ⓑ Ⓒ Ⓓ
3. Ⓐ Ⓑ Ⓒ Ⓓ

Lesson 14
Student Practice
1. Ⓐ Ⓑ Ⓒ Ⓓ
2. Ⓐ Ⓑ Ⓒ Ⓓ
3. Ⓐ Ⓑ Ⓒ Ⓓ
4. Ⓐ Ⓑ Ⓒ Ⓓ

Transparency
1. Ⓐ Ⓑ Ⓒ Ⓓ
2. Ⓐ Ⓑ Ⓒ Ⓓ
3. Ⓐ Ⓑ Ⓒ Ⓓ

Lesson 16
Student Practice
1. Ⓐ Ⓑ Ⓒ Ⓓ
2. Ⓐ Ⓑ Ⓒ Ⓓ
3. Ⓐ Ⓑ Ⓒ Ⓓ
4. Ⓐ Ⓑ Ⓒ Ⓓ

Transparency
1. Ⓐ Ⓑ Ⓒ Ⓓ
2. Ⓐ Ⓑ Ⓒ Ⓓ

Lesson 17
Student Practice
1. Ⓐ Ⓑ Ⓒ Ⓓ
2. Ⓐ Ⓑ Ⓒ Ⓓ
3. Ⓐ Ⓑ Ⓒ Ⓓ
4. Ⓐ Ⓑ Ⓒ Ⓓ

Transparency
1. Ⓐ Ⓑ Ⓒ Ⓓ
2. Ⓐ Ⓑ Ⓒ Ⓓ
3. Ⓐ Ⓑ Ⓒ Ⓓ

Lesson 18
Student Practice
1. Ⓐ Ⓑ Ⓒ Ⓓ
2. Ⓐ Ⓑ Ⓒ Ⓓ
3. Ⓐ Ⓑ Ⓒ Ⓓ

Transparency
1. Ⓐ Ⓑ Ⓒ Ⓓ
2. Ⓐ Ⓑ Ⓒ Ⓓ
3. Ⓐ Ⓑ Ⓒ Ⓓ

Lesson 19
Student Practice
1. Ⓐ Ⓑ Ⓒ Ⓓ
2. Ⓐ Ⓑ Ⓒ Ⓓ
3. Ⓐ Ⓑ Ⓒ Ⓓ
4. Ⓐ Ⓑ Ⓒ Ⓓ
5. Ⓐ Ⓑ Ⓒ Ⓓ
6. Ⓐ Ⓑ Ⓒ Ⓓ

Transparency
1. Ⓐ Ⓑ Ⓒ Ⓓ
2. Ⓐ Ⓑ Ⓒ Ⓓ
3. Ⓐ Ⓑ Ⓒ Ⓓ

Lesson 21
Student Practice
1. Ⓐ Ⓑ Ⓒ Ⓓ
2. Ⓐ Ⓑ Ⓒ Ⓓ
3. Ⓐ Ⓑ Ⓒ Ⓓ

Transparency
1. Ⓐ Ⓑ Ⓒ Ⓓ
2. Ⓐ Ⓑ Ⓒ Ⓓ
3. Ⓐ Ⓑ Ⓒ Ⓓ

Lesson 22
Student Practice
1. Ⓐ Ⓑ Ⓒ Ⓓ
2. Ⓐ Ⓑ Ⓒ Ⓓ
3. Ⓐ Ⓑ Ⓒ Ⓓ

Transparency
1. Ⓐ Ⓑ Ⓒ Ⓓ
2. Ⓐ Ⓑ Ⓒ Ⓓ
3. Ⓐ Ⓑ Ⓒ Ⓓ

Lesson 23
Student Practice
1. Ⓐ Ⓑ Ⓒ Ⓓ
2. Ⓐ Ⓑ Ⓒ Ⓓ
3. Ⓐ Ⓑ Ⓒ Ⓓ
4. Ⓐ Ⓑ Ⓒ Ⓓ
5. Ⓐ Ⓑ Ⓒ Ⓓ

Transparency
1. Ⓐ Ⓑ Ⓒ Ⓓ
2. Ⓐ Ⓑ Ⓒ Ⓓ
3. Ⓐ Ⓑ Ⓒ Ⓓ

Lesson 24
Student Practice
1. Ⓐ Ⓑ Ⓒ Ⓓ
2. Ⓐ Ⓑ Ⓒ Ⓓ
3. Ⓐ Ⓑ Ⓒ Ⓓ
4. Ⓐ Ⓑ Ⓒ Ⓓ

Transparency
1. Ⓐ Ⓑ Ⓒ Ⓓ
2. Ⓐ Ⓑ Ⓒ Ⓓ
3. Ⓐ Ⓑ Ⓒ Ⓓ

Name _____ Date _____

OCCT Test Preparation

Lesson 26
Student Practice
1. Ⓐ Ⓑ Ⓒ Ⓓ
2. Ⓐ Ⓑ Ⓒ Ⓓ
3. Ⓐ Ⓑ Ⓒ Ⓓ

Transparency
1. Ⓐ Ⓑ Ⓒ Ⓓ
2. Ⓐ Ⓑ Ⓒ Ⓓ
3. Ⓐ Ⓑ Ⓒ Ⓓ

Lesson 28
Student Practice
1. Ⓐ Ⓑ Ⓒ Ⓓ
2. Ⓐ Ⓑ Ⓒ Ⓓ
3. Ⓐ Ⓑ Ⓒ Ⓓ

Transparency
1. Ⓐ Ⓑ Ⓒ Ⓓ
2. Ⓐ Ⓑ Ⓒ Ⓓ

Lesson 27
Student Practice
1. Ⓐ Ⓑ Ⓒ Ⓓ
2. Ⓐ Ⓑ Ⓒ Ⓓ
3. Ⓐ Ⓑ Ⓒ Ⓓ
4. Ⓐ Ⓑ Ⓒ Ⓓ

Transparency
1. Ⓐ Ⓑ Ⓒ Ⓓ
2. Ⓐ Ⓑ Ⓒ Ⓓ
3. Ⓐ Ⓑ Ⓒ Ⓓ

Lesson 29
Student Practice
1. Ⓐ Ⓑ Ⓒ Ⓓ
2. Ⓐ Ⓑ Ⓒ Ⓓ
3. Ⓐ Ⓑ Ⓒ Ⓓ

Transparency
1. Ⓐ Ⓑ Ⓒ Ⓓ
2. Ⓐ Ⓑ Ⓒ Ⓓ
3. Ⓐ Ⓑ Ⓒ Ⓓ

Answer Document — **OCCT Test Preparation**

Name _____ Date _____

OCCT Reading Practice Test 1

Here is a list with pictures to help you locate the selections in your Reading Practice Test. The questions follow each selection.

Carmen's Diary .... Page 73

The Disappearing Cat .... Page 78

Pepitas: A Tasty Autumn Snack .... Page 83

Horsing Around Riding Center .... Page 88

Ask the Fish Doctor .... Page 92

Brush Strokes .... Page 97

My Brother, the Polar Bear .... Page 101

A New Holiday .... Page 103

Dear Mandy .... Page 105

The Esophagus .... Page 107

Writing Practice Test .... Page 111

GO ON ▶

Read the selection below. Then answer the questions that follow.

Carmen's Diary

by Carmen Rodriguez

May 17
Dear Diary,

1   I had a wonderful day! Our teacher took the entire class to the Concord Butterfly Museum. The whole museum is about butterflies. I thought I already knew all there is to know about butterflies. We studied them in science class with Mr. Neller. I was surprised by how much new information I learned on our field trip.

2   We met our museum guide as soon as we stepped off the bus. She handed each of us a worksheet called "The Great Museum Challenge." It had a list of clues that we had to follow to find the answers to the questions. It was like a treasure hunt inside the museum.

3   Next, our class divided up into pairs. Our guide gave us maps of the museum and told us that we could answer the questions in any order. She said that we could ask her or our teacher for help. She also said that we should try our best to answer all of the questions on our own. I was excited to begin, because I love playing detective and solving mysteries.

4   My partner was Raul. We decided to start with the first question, which

GO ON

asked, "What is the largest butterfly in the world?" The clue was a picture of a queen wearing a crown. Raul is good at understanding hints. He said that we should look for something with the word "queen" on it. I am good at using maps to find places. I looked at the museum map and saw that one room had a display called "Amazing Butterfly Facts." I led us there.

5   As soon as we walked into the room, Raul spotted a sign that said "Meet the Queen of Butterflies." We knew we had found the answer to the first question. The display showed a butterfly called Queen Alexandra's Birdwing. With its wings open, it was eleven inches wide! I was delighted that we had answered our first question.

6   After we wrote down the answer, we chose our next question. It said, "A butterfly and a moth may look the same, but they are very different.

What is one difference?" The clue was a picture of the Sun. Raul and I discussed this clue. We both said what we thought it meant. Then, he said that we should try to find a display that compared butterflies and moths.

7   I looked at the map and saw a display called "Butterflies and Other Insects." It was in an odd part of the museum. I followed the map closely, and soon Raul and I found what we were looking for. We later learned that some of our classmates spent much time trying to find their way through the museum to the display. When Raul and I reached the display, we saw that one of the glass cases had a sign on it that said "Moths." We read the information, and then the clue made sense! We learned that butterflies fly during the day, when the Sun is out. Moths usually fly at night.

8   Raul and I were able to answer all of the questions on our worksheet by working together. When we finished, I cheered and gave him a high-five. Then, we went into the last room, which turned out to be our favorite. Displays of hundreds of beautiful butterflies filled the room. Tomorrow I will tell Carla all about the museum.

1 Which is the best definition of <u>discussed</u>?

A asked about
B talked about
C disagreed about
D wondered about

2 What is the <u>first</u> event in the diary entry that tells the reader that Carmen enjoyed the butterfly museum?

A Carmen loved playing detective and solving mysteries.
B Carmen was delighted when she solved the first question.
C Carmen looked forward to telling Carla all about the museum.
D Carmen had a wonderful day at the Concord Butterfly Museum.

3 What did Carmen's class do <u>after</u> they received the worksheets?

A They went to the museum.
B They walked off of the bus.
C They formed groups of two.
D They met the museum guide.

4 Which two words from the diary have almost the same meaning?

A clues, hints
B question, detective
C maps, places
D beautiful, warm

5 How are butterflies different from moths?

A Butterflies move by flying, and moths move by walking.
B Butterflies like warm places, and moths like cold places.
C Butterflies fly during the day, and moths fly at night.
D Butterflies are usually large, and most moths are small.

6 What is the name of the display that helps Carmen and Raul answer the second question?

A "Amazing Butterfly Facts"
B "Butterflies and Other Insects"
C "Moths and Butterflies"
D "Concord Butterfly Museum"

GO ON ▶

7 Why does Carmen plan to tell Carla about the butterfly museum?

A Carmen wants to know which display Carla liked best.

B Carmen usually goes on treasure hunts with Carla.

C Carmen knows that Carla likes museums.

D Carmen enjoyed her trip to the museum.

8 How are Raul and Carmen different?

A Carmen likes museums, but Raul does not.

B Carmen is good at using maps, and Raul is good at understanding clues.

C Raul knows a great deal about butterflies, but Carmen does not.

D Raul thinks moths fly at night, but Carmen thinks they fly during the day.

Read the selection below. Then answer the questions that follow.

The Disappearing Cat
by Samantha Brown

1   Tyrell sighed. He had not seen Squeaker for an entire day. He wondered how he would explain to his mother that he lost his cat. He lifted the edge of his bedspread and peered under the bed. As he <u>inspected</u> the rest of the house, he thought about the months since Squeaker had joined his family.

* * *

2   Squeaker had appeared one summer morning when Tyrell and his mother were eating breakfast on the porch. It was a beautiful day, and Tyrell thought that he would ask his mother whether he could invite a friend over to play. At that moment she put down her fork and closed her eyes.

3   "Did you hear that?" she asked. Tyrell listened, and then he heard a squeaky *mee mee mee* sound coming from the bushes near the door. He opened the door and came outside. A small brown cat with dark stripes hopped up on the step beside him. The cat looked up at him and squeaked again, *mee mee mee*. Every other cat Tyrell had met said *meow*, not *mee mee mee*. He knew right away that he would name the cat Squeaker.

4   Squeaker visited their house every day that summer. Every morning, she hopped up on the step and let Tyrell pet her. Tyrell's mother started leaving food and water outside for her. Squeaker spent the days napping in the bushes. At night, she disappeared, but she always returned the next morning.

5   Summer turned into autumn, and the nights grew cooler. One cold, windy evening, Tyrell looked outside and saw Squeaker waiting patiently on the front step. Tyrell showed this to his mother. She went outside and opened the door, and Squeaker ran inside. After that, Squeaker spent every night curled up in front of the stove.

GO ON ▶

6   Tyrell could tell that Squeaker was happy living in their house. She began eating more food, and she grew larger as the weeks went by. When Tyrell picked her up, he noticed that she was heavier. He was pleased that she was so strong and healthy.

* * *

7   Tyrell felt ready to give up looking for Squeaker. Over the past week, he had noticed that she seemed to be looking for new places to hide. Once, he found her in the cabinet under the kitchen sink. The next day, she made herself a bed in a pile of dirty clothes in the bathroom. He checked both of these places. Then, he sat down on the stairs and put his head in his hands.

8   Suddenly, he heard a familiar noise, a squeaky *mee mee mee*. Tyrell followed the noise to his mother's closet and opened the door. He could hear Squeaker, but he couldn't see her. He crawled all the way to the back of the closet, behind his mother's suitcases. Squeaker was curled up on an old coat that had fallen off its hanger. Tyrell grinned and petted her.

9   Squeaker started purring, but Tyrell could still hear the squeaking, *mee mee mee*. He looked closer and saw three tiny kittens huddled next to her. He touched one lightly, and all three began squeaking with excitement. He thought about how Squeaker had grown larger over the last few weeks and how she had disappeared.

10 "You didn't disappear," he said to Squeaker. "You just needed a safe place to have your kittens." Squeaker purred. Tyrell patted her, and then he raced downstairs to tell his mother the good news about his disappearing cat.

GO ON ▶

9 Which word has nearly the same meaning as <u>inspected</u>?

A searched
B measured
C surrounded
D remembered

10 Why did the author write the story "The Disappearing Cat"?

A to persuade readers to buy a pet cat
B to entertain readers with a happy story
C to help people locate their missing pets
D to give information about caring for cats

11 What is Tyrell's <u>biggest</u> problem in the story?

A His mother wants him to give Squeaker away.
B He is unable to find Squeaker in the house.
C His mother is against leaving food and water for Squeaker.
D He doubts that he can care for Squeaker's kittens.

GO ON ▶

12 How is Squeaker **different** from other cats?

A She enjoys being petted.
B She dislikes cold weather.
C She spends the day napping.
D She makes an unusual sound.

13 How does Tyrell finally solve his problem?

A He calls out Squeaker's name many times.
B He asks his mother to look in her bedroom.
C He follows the squeaking sound to the closet.
D He looks under the bushes by the front door.

14 Why does Tyrell's mother allow Squeaker into the house?

A The weather is too cold for Squeaker to stay outside.
B She wants to stop Squeaker from disappearing at night.
C She thinks that Tyrell needs a pet to keep him company.
D The cat keeps squeaking loudly and pawing at the front door.

GO ON ▶

15. What does the word <u>huddled</u> mean the way it's used in the story?

A moving all together
B lying close together
C making loud noises
D sleeping very deeply

16. Which character in the story says, "You just needed a safe place to have your kittens"?

A Squeaker
B Tyrell's mother
C Tyrell
D Tyrell's father

Read the selection below. Then answer the questions that follow.

Pepitas: A Tasty Autumn Snack

by Juan Menendez

What You Need:

1   Pepitas, or roasted pumpkin seeds, are easy to make and delicious to eat. This salty, crunchy treat is also a healthy snack. First, ask an adult to help you. Then, gather all the foods and tools on the list below. Ask the adult to find the kitchen knife.

Foods	Tools
• one pumpkin • olive oil • salt	• a strainer • measuring cups and spoons • a large bowl • a baking sheet • oven • kitchen knife

2   **Directions: Follow the steps and the diagram below to make pepitas.**

3   To begin preparing the pepitas, ask an adult to <u>preheat</u> the oven to 300°F. This will allow the oven time to heat up. Then, ask an adult to cut off the top of the pumpkin. The hole should be large enough so that you can fit your hand inside. Next, use your hands or a large spoon to scoop out all of the seeds.

4   After you remove the seeds, you need to wash them. Place the seeds in a strainer, or a bowl with small holes in the bottom. Because the seeds are larger than the holes, the seeds will stay in the bowl, but the water will drain out. Rinse the seeds with cold water until they are clean.

5   Next, use a measuring cup to count how many cups of seeds you have. Then, measure 1 tablespoon of olive oil and $\frac{1}{2}$ teaspoon of salt for every cup of seeds you have. For example, if you have 2 cups of seeds, then you need 2 tablespoons of olive oil and 1 teaspoon of salt. An adult can help you measure.

GO ON ▶

6   Next, mix the oil and the seeds together in a large bowl. Make sure that all of the seeds are coated with oil. Then, spread the seeds in one layer on the baking sheet. Finally, lightly sprinkle salt over the seeds. Now you are ready to bake pepitas!

7   Have an adult place the baking sheet in the oven. The seeds should bake for about 45 minutes. An adult needs to stir the seeds every 5 minutes so that they do not burn. You will know when the seeds are done because they will be brown and crispy.

8   After the seeds have finished cooking, have an adult remove them from the oven. Allow the seeds to cool, and then enjoy a delicious snack!

9   **This diagram shows nine steps you can follow to make pepitas.**

Step 1 Have an adult preheat the oven to 300°F.		**Step 2** Remove the seeds and wash them.		**Step 3** Measure the seeds.
Step 6 Spread the seeds on the baking sheet.		**Step 5** Mix the oil and the seeds together in a large bowl.	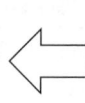	**Step 4** Measure the oil and salt.
Step 7 Lightly sprinkle the salt over the seeds.		**Step 8** Have an adult bake and stir the seeds.		**Step 9** Allow the seeds to cool, and enjoy your tasty and healthy snack!

GO ON ▶

17 In the selection, what does the word <u>preheat</u> mean?

A heat often
B heat less
C heat in advance
D heat again

18 Based on the diagram, what tool do you need to complete Step 2?

A strainer
B a large bowl
C a baking sheet
D measuring cups

19 What should you do <u>before</u> you count how many cups of seeds you have?

A Sprinkle salt over the seeds.
B Wait until the seeds have cooled.
C Stir the oil and the seeds together.
D Take the seeds out of the pumpkin.

GO ON ▶

20. Which statement would the author of "Pepitas: A Tasty Autumn Snack" *most likely* agree with?

A Pepitas have a taste that most people dislike.

B Children usually like pepitas better than other snacks.

C Pepitas are more popular today than in the past.

D Children should use an oven only with an adult's help.

21. Based on the diagram and the story, why do the seeds need to be stirred in step 8?

A to make them turn brown

B to give them a salty taste

C to keep them from burning

D to coat them evenly with oil

22. Why do you need to measure how many cups of seeds you have?

A to find the correct oven temperature for the seeds

B to know how long you need to bake the seeds

C to decide what size baking sheet you must use

D to learn the amount of oil and salt you will need

GO ON ▶

23 In the selection, what does the word sprinkle mean?

A heat
B dust
C shake
D divide

24 Why did the author write "Pepitas: A Tasty Autumn Snack"?

A to explain the history of pepitas
B to show that pepitas are a healthy snack
C to teach readers how to make pepitas
D to teach readers how to cut open a pumpkin

STOP

Read the selection below. Then answer the questions that follow.

Horsing Around Riding Center
We make riding fun!

Do you love horses? Have you always wanted to learn to ride? If so, then come to Horsing Around Riding Center!

Horsing Around Riding Center is a place where people of all ages can have fun while becoming better riders. Horsing Around has classes for both beginning and <u>advanced</u> riders. We offer the following classes for beginning riders:

Age	Class
6 to 8	Peanuts on Ponies
8 to 12	Kids Can Ride
12 to 18	Terrific Teens
Over 18	Adult Adventurers

Call, write, or visit us to learn about our other riding classes.

Contact Us!

Horsing Around Riding Center
15 Morgan Lane
Holbrook, New Hampshire 33950
(634) 667–4435
www.horsingaroundriding.com

> "I was afraid to ride at first, but I relaxed during my <u>initial</u> lesson and had fun. Soon I was <u>fearless</u>. I enjoyed every lesson after that, too. This is the best place to learn to ride!"
>
> *Maya Jonas, age 12*

GO ON ▶

25

Why does the author ask questions at the top of the selection?

A to make readers interested in the ad

B to share the success of one young rider

C to tell where the riding center is located

D to give readers information about classes

26

Who can take the class called "Peanuts on Ponies"?

A all levels of riders ages six to eight

B all levels of riders over eighteen

C beginning riders ages six to eight

D beginning riders of all ages

27

What does the word <u>advanced</u> mean the way it's used in this selection?

A skilled

B average

C busy

D young

GO ON ▶

28 What does the word <u>fearless</u> mean?

A causing fear
B needing fear
C with much fear
D without fear

29 What statement would the author of "Horsing Around Riding Center" <u>most likely</u> agree with?

A You should learn to ride on horseback in order to make new friends.
B Both new and experienced riders can have fun with horses.
C Young people are usually interested in learning new things.
D Most people enjoy doing something that they have never done before.

30 Which word means nearly the <u>opposite</u> of <u>initial</u>?

A final
B better
C recent
D exciting

GO ON ▶

31 How are the "Kids Can Ride" and "Terrific Teens" classes alike?

A Both classes are meant for advanced riders only.

B They are both for riders between the ages of twelve and eighteen.

C Both classes allow riders of all ages to take part.

D They are both for people without much riding experience.

32 What is the author's purpose for writing "Horsing Around Riding Center"?

A to give people facts about horseback riding

B to entertain people with a story about riding horses

C to persuade people to sign up for horse riding lessons

D to tell people how Maya Jones felt about her first lesson

Read the selection below. Then answer the questions that follow.

Ask the Fish Doctor
by Dr. Aisha Lamont

Meet Dr. Lamont

1   Hello! My name is Dr. Aisha Lamont. People call me a "fish doctor" because I heal sick fish as part of my work. I grew up in Iowa, a state that is far from any ocean. As a child, I dreamed of living by the sea. My parents owned a farm, and I loved spending time with all kinds of animals. I chose a job that allowed me to study animals and the ocean at the same time. I love my work.

2   As part of my work, I visit schools to teach children about fish. Children ask me questions that many people would find interesting. I decided to write a weekly question-and-answer article so that students from all over the world could get answers to their questions about fish.

Question of the Week:

3   This week's question comes from Anthony Myers in Havre, Montana. Anthony is in the fourth grade at Havre Elementary School. Here is Anthony's question:

Dear Dr. Lamont,

4   My class has two pet fish named Greta and Bob. We observe them to learn about fish. We know what they eat and how they swim, but we have one question that we can't answer. Do fish sleep?

Sincerely,
Anthony Myers

GO ON ▶

Do Fish Sleep?

5   What a good question, Anthony! You may be surprised by my answer, which is, "yes and no." The answer is *no* because fish do not sleep in the same way that people and other animals sleep. When people sleep, they close their eyes. Most fish cannot do this, because they do not have eyelids.

6   But the answer to your question is also *yes*. All fish rest in one way or another, and resting is kind of like sleep. Some fish even lie down on the ocean floor! Others hide among plants or rocks and remain still for long periods of time. Some fish are active during the day and rest at night. Other fish are like cats; they rest during much of the day and stay awake at night. If you notice that Greta and Bob are active during the day, when you are in school, then they probably rest at night.

7   Some fish are unable to stop swimming because they must swim in order to breathe. They breathe by moving water through parts of their bodies called *gills*. If you watch these fish, you will notice that they sometimes swim very slowly and look like they are "daydreaming." Scientists think that this is a way of sleeping and moving at the same time!

8   Scientists still have much to learn about fish, including the way they sleep. Fish and people have something in common: we all need our rest! Thank you for your question, and be sure to keep reading "Ask the Fish Doctor" to learn more about these wonderful creatures.

33 Which phrase has nearly the same meaning as heal?

A help cure
B study closely
C keep as pets
D show to others

35 Which word has the same root as unable?

A depend
B unsure
C disable
D uneasy

34 Why did Anthony Myers write to Dr. Lamont?

A to tell Dr. Lamont about his class's two pet fish
B to invite Dr. Lamont to speak to his science class
C to find out when Greta and Bob should be sleeping
D to ask a question that his class was unable to answer

GO ON ▶

36

Why are some types of fish compared to cats in the story?

A They are unable to close their eyes.

B They enjoy spending time in water.

C They have special ways of breathing.

D They spend much of the day resting.

37

Why do some fish have to keep moving at all times?

A They never need to rest their bodies.

B They have to escape from other fish.

C They can breathe only while moving.

D They must travel long distances to feed.

GO ON ▶

38 Which reason best tells why the author wrote this article?

A to give readers information about fish

B to persuade young people to study fish

C to show readers how to care for their fish

D to tell a story from the author's childhood years

39 Which reason best explains why Dr. Lamont decided to become a "fish doctor"?

A because she likes studying animals on her parents' farm

B because she loves the ocean

C because she wanted to study animals and the ocean at the same time

D because she grew up in Iowa

Read the selection below. Then answer the questions below.

Brush Strokes

by David Mann Jr.

1   This month, Sonya's art class was learning about painting. Last month, they had studied pottery. Sonya had decided pottery was her favorite form of art. She loved the feeling of wet, sticky clay between her fingers. She was amazed that she could turn a lump of clay into something beautiful that people could use.

2   Sonya had made her father a large bowl that she painted bright green. He used it to serve food, such as salad or popcorn. Sonya believed that nothing could be as much fun as the pottery unit had been. She watched her teacher, Mr. Watson, unroll a poster on his desk, and she yawned.

3   "I'm going to show you one of my favorite works of art," said Mr. Watson. "When I first saw this, I knew that I wanted to be a painter." He tacked a large poster on the board in the front of the room. Sonya looked up, and her eyes opened wide.

4   The painting showed a night sky that was lit up by the moon and many stars. Under the sky was a village with houses surrounded by trees and mountains. A group of thin, tall trees stretched up the left side of the painting. The trees were black, and the stars and the moon were bright yellow. Everything else was painted in shades of blue. Sonya had never seen a painting like it before. She loved it.

5   "I want to show you this painting because we just finished our unit on pottery. If you look at it closely, you can see each and every brush stroke. This artist used paint almost like a potter uses clay. He painted in thick layers, which made the surface of the painting raised and bumpy."

6   "I know that some of you are disappointed that the pottery unit

GO ON ▶

is over," Mr. Watson said. He looked at Sonya as he spoke. "I hope that this painting shows you that different forms of art have much in common. We will study many painting styles, and you can choose the style that works best for you."

7 Sonya gazed at the poster. She imagined herself painting her favorite place, the ocean. Like this painting, hers would show each and every brush stroke. That way, she could show the colors and movements of the ocean water. She could paint the light sparkling on the waves. Sonya could hardly wait to begin. She sat up straight and listened carefully to Mr. Watson. She did not want to miss one second of the painting unit.

40 Which word has the same root as painter?

A potter
B reader
C patient
D repaint

41 Why does Sonya open her eyes wide when she sees the painting?

A She is trying not to fall asleep in class.
B She is surprised that she likes the painting.
C She is having a hard time seeing the poster.
D She is thinking that she has seen the painting before.

42 Why does Mr. Watson compare the artist who made the poster to a potter?

A The artist mixed paint and clay together.
B The artist made many paintings of pottery.
C The artist made things that people could use.
D The artist used large amounts of paint like clay.

GO ON ▶

43

Why does Mr. Watson look at Sonya when he describes the poster?

A He wants to know whether Sonya likes the painting's colors.

B He wants to make sure that Sonya is paying attention in class.

C He knows that Sonya is sad because the pottery unit has ended.

D He knows that one of Sonya's favorite artists did the painting.

44

How are Sonya and Mr. Watson alike?

A Both have their own styles of painting.

B Both enjoy painting pictures of the ocean.

C Both would rather make pottery than a painting.

D Both like the painting on the poster.

45

What is Sonya's main problem in the story?

A The painting unit, her favorite, has ended.

B Mr. Watson doesn't like pottery.

C The pottery unit, her favorite, has ended.

D She likes painting more than pottery.

STOP

Practice 1 — Reading Practice Test

Name _____ Date _____

Read the selection below. Then answer the questions that follow.

My Brother, the Polar Bear

1 My brother's favorite thing to do is to swim. His favorite time of the year is summer, because he can go swimming every day. Each year, he waits impatiently for the first day that is warm enough for swimming. Then, he begs our father to take him to Uncle Mark's house, which is on a lake.

2 This spring, the weather stayed cool much longer that it usually does. One cold, windy afternoon my father and brother were going to see Uncle Mark. I asked whether I could join the two of them. As soon as we arrived, my brother jumped out of the car, ran across the yard, and dove into the lake! Can you believe it?

GO ON ▶

46 The author compares his brother to a polar bear because his brother

A likes to play in the snow.
B swam in cold water.
C is big and hairy.
D enjoys wintertime.

47 What was the author's purpose in writing this selection?

A to show readers pictures of polar bears
B to give readers facts about swimming
C to entertain readers with a fun story
D to inform readers about polar bears

48 With which sentence would the author most likely agree?

A Polar bears are the most interesting animals in the world.
B Swimming is my favorite sport.
C My brother hates swimming.
D Swimming in cold water is for polar bears.

STOP

Read the selection below. Then answer the questions that follow.

A New Holiday

1   Every year on the Fourth of July, my whole family gets together. We eat special foods, play games, and watch fireworks at night. The best part of the day is seeing all of my cousins. Many of them live far away, and I only see them on a few special days each year.

2   This year's Fourth of July party was the best ever. The day went by too quickly, and suddenly it was time for the fireworks. After that, my cousins and their families had to go home. I was very disappointed, because I knew it would be a long time before the next holiday.

3   Then, I came up with a great idea. I ran up to my room and took out paper and markers. I made a huge sign that said "Happy Fifth of July," and I hung it in the kitchen.

4   My mother laughed. She said that she sometimes wished that every day could be a holiday, so she could always be with her family. She told me that my cousins could not make the long trip to our house the next day. Then she said that we could celebrate the new holiday together. We planned to eat a special dinner and play games together.

GO ON ▶

49 What was the author's purpose in writing this selection?

A to inform readers about holidays

B to entertain readers with an interesting story

C to give readers facts about traditions

D to teach readers how to make banners

50 What inference can you make about the way the author's cousins felt at the end of the second paragraph?

A They were happy that the author wanted them to stay longer.

B They were disappointed that the author made a banner for them.

C They were sad to be leaving the author's house.

D They were disappointed that they were missing the Fifth of July party.

51 Why did the author create a Fifth of July party banner?

A because the author's cousins couldn't come to the Fourth of July party

B to give the author's cousins a reason to return

C because the author's cousins wanted a new reason to celebrate

D to give the author's mom a reason to make another cake

STOP

Read the selection below. Then answer the questions that follow.

15 Laurel Hill Road
Cedar Grove, ME 22877
May 17, 2007

Dear Mandy,

1   Are you having fun on your trip? I'm sure your grandparents are happy that you came to visit, and Pennsylvania sounds like a fun place. The Philadelphia Zoo sounds especially amazing. I can't wait to see your pictures when you return home in two weeks.

2   It's too bad that you were not here at summer camp yesterday, because our topic was water. It might sound boring, but it wasn't! We made crafts and played games that all had to do with water. We have a new camper in our group, and his name is Carl.

3   First, we learned about how water turns into clouds and makes rain, and then we did an art project. Mr. Chen had us draw pictures to show each step. I had to draw a picture of a rain cloud, and I made a huge cloud that was dark gray. After we finished, we displayed our pictures in order on the wall.

4   We went outside, and Mr. Chen taught us a game called "Raindrops and Sun Rays." Most of us were raindrops, and three people were sun rays. I was a raindrop, and I had to stay away from the sun rays. If I was tagged by a sun ray, then I would "dry up," and be out of the game.

5   After the game, we were all feeling hot, so Mr. Chen set up the sprinkler for us to run through. We also cooled off by drinking cold water, and Mr. Chen reminded us that we should drink extra water on hot days.

6   Tomorrow's topic is music. I'll write you another letter to tell you all about it. Have fun with your grandparents, and tell them I say hello!

Your friend,
Connor

GO ON

52

What is the genre of this selection?

A letter
B dictionary entry
C story
D nonfiction article

53

What is the main idea of this selection?

A Connor is informing Mandy about his day at camp.
B Connor is telling Mandy facts about rain.
C Connor is entertaining Mandy with a story.
D Connor is persuading Mandy to come home.

54

What is the first thing Connor did with Mr. Chen?

A Connor learned about how water turns into clouds and makes rain.
B Connor drew each step of the water cycle.
C Mr. Chen taught Connor a game called "Raindrops and Sun Rays."
D Mr. Chen set up a sprinkler.

STOP

OCCT Test Preparation Page 106 Reading Practice Test

Food travels to the stomach through the esophagus. Muscles at each end control openings that allow food in and out.

Read the selection below. Then answer the questions that follow.

The Esophagus

1   After food is swallowed, it travels to the stomach. It moves through a long tube called the esophagus. The tube can expand, or get wider. It can also contract, or get narrower. Expanding and contracting allow food to move through it. The tube is in front of the spinal column. It is behind the heart and the trachea, or windpipe.

2   The top and bottom of the esophagus has muscles that open and close. The top is usually closed. It opens to let food in the throat pass through the tube. Then, it closes so too much food cannot go in at once. Muscles in the tube's wall move food downward. This process is called *peristalsis*.

3   When food reaches the bottom of the tube, muscles allow it through into the stomach. The muscles close the opening quickly. That keeps gastric juices and partly digested food in the stomach from going into the esophagus. If gastric juices do enter the esophagus, it causes the discomfort known as heartburn.

GO ON ▶

55 Gastric juices entering the esophagus can cause

A contractions.
B peristalsis.
C heartburn.
D tracheas.

56 What does the word discomfort mean?

A uneasiness
B illness
C experience
D reaction

57 How is the esophagus different from the trachea?

A The esophagus is also called "windpipe."
B The esophagus produces gastric juices.
C The esophagus allows food to move through it.
D The esophagus allows air to move through it.

58 Based on the article, you know that the esophagus

A is connected to the stomach.
B is made of bone.
C is located in front of the heart.
D is shaped like triangle.

59 You would most likely find this article in

A an atlas.
B a collection of short stories.
C an encyclopedia.
D a book of poetry.

60 The author wrote this article mainly to

A inform readers about the cure for heartburn.
B compare different organs of the digestive system.
C explain how the esophagus works.
D persuade the reader to eat healthier food.

ANSWER DOCUMENT

Name _____ Date _____

1. Ⓐ Ⓑ Ⓒ Ⓓ
2. Ⓐ Ⓑ Ⓒ Ⓓ
3. Ⓐ Ⓑ Ⓒ Ⓓ
4. Ⓐ Ⓑ Ⓒ Ⓓ
5. Ⓐ Ⓑ Ⓒ Ⓓ
6. Ⓐ Ⓑ Ⓒ Ⓓ
7. Ⓐ Ⓑ Ⓒ Ⓓ
8. Ⓐ Ⓑ Ⓒ Ⓓ

9. Ⓐ Ⓑ Ⓒ Ⓓ
10. Ⓐ Ⓑ Ⓒ Ⓓ
11. Ⓐ Ⓑ Ⓒ Ⓓ
12. Ⓐ Ⓑ Ⓒ Ⓓ
13. Ⓐ Ⓑ Ⓒ Ⓓ
14. Ⓐ Ⓑ Ⓒ Ⓓ
15. Ⓐ Ⓑ Ⓒ Ⓓ
16. Ⓐ Ⓑ Ⓒ Ⓓ

17. Ⓐ Ⓑ Ⓒ Ⓓ
18. Ⓐ Ⓑ Ⓒ Ⓓ
19. Ⓐ Ⓑ Ⓒ Ⓓ
20. Ⓐ Ⓑ Ⓒ Ⓓ
21. Ⓐ Ⓑ Ⓒ Ⓓ
22. Ⓐ Ⓑ Ⓒ Ⓓ
23. Ⓐ Ⓑ Ⓒ Ⓓ
24. Ⓐ Ⓑ Ⓒ Ⓓ

25. Ⓐ Ⓑ Ⓒ Ⓓ
26. Ⓐ Ⓑ Ⓒ Ⓓ
27. Ⓐ Ⓑ Ⓒ Ⓓ
28. Ⓐ Ⓑ Ⓒ Ⓓ
29. Ⓐ Ⓑ Ⓒ Ⓓ
30. Ⓐ Ⓑ Ⓒ Ⓓ
31. Ⓐ Ⓑ Ⓒ Ⓓ
32. Ⓐ Ⓑ Ⓒ Ⓓ

33. Ⓐ Ⓑ Ⓒ Ⓓ
34. Ⓐ Ⓑ Ⓒ Ⓓ
35. Ⓐ Ⓑ Ⓒ Ⓓ
36. Ⓐ Ⓑ Ⓒ Ⓓ
37. Ⓐ Ⓑ Ⓒ Ⓓ
38. Ⓐ Ⓑ Ⓒ Ⓓ
39. Ⓐ Ⓑ Ⓒ Ⓓ

40. Ⓐ Ⓑ Ⓒ Ⓓ
41. Ⓐ Ⓑ Ⓒ Ⓓ
42. Ⓐ Ⓑ Ⓒ Ⓓ
43. Ⓐ Ⓑ Ⓒ Ⓓ
44. Ⓐ Ⓑ Ⓒ Ⓓ
45. Ⓐ Ⓑ Ⓒ Ⓓ

46. Ⓐ Ⓑ Ⓒ Ⓓ
47. Ⓐ Ⓑ Ⓒ Ⓓ
48. Ⓐ Ⓑ Ⓒ Ⓓ

49. Ⓐ Ⓑ Ⓒ Ⓓ
50. Ⓐ Ⓑ Ⓒ Ⓓ
51. Ⓐ Ⓑ Ⓒ Ⓓ

52. Ⓐ Ⓑ Ⓒ Ⓓ
53. Ⓐ Ⓑ Ⓒ Ⓓ
54. Ⓐ Ⓑ Ⓒ Ⓓ

55. Ⓐ Ⓑ Ⓒ Ⓓ
56. Ⓐ Ⓑ Ⓒ Ⓓ
57. Ⓐ Ⓑ Ⓒ Ⓓ
58. Ⓐ Ⓑ Ⓒ Ⓓ
59. Ⓐ Ⓑ Ⓒ Ⓓ
60. Ⓐ Ⓑ Ⓒ Ⓓ

OCCT Writing Practice Test 1

Today you will write a composition on an assigned topic. Your writing will be scored on how fully you develop the topic and on how well you organize and express your ideas. Your composition will be scored by trained readers. As you work, keep in mind these three stages of the writing process:

- **Planning**: Take time to plan your writing by listing, outlining, or organizing your ideas in the space provided.

- **Writing**: Write about the topic in a clear and logical manner on the five lined pages following the *Planning Page.* You do not need to use all of the pages, but make sure your composition is as complete as possible. Be sure to include a beginning, a middle, and an ending for your composition.

- **Editing/Revising**: Take time to reread what you have written, and decide if you need to add more details or change the organization of your composition. At the same time, look for and correct any errors in grammar, punctuation, capitalization, and spelling. You may use the *Writer's Checklist* to help you revise your writing.

Most students will be able to complete the writing task within about 50 minutes, but you may take up to one extra hour to complete your test. Try to budget your time wisely so you will have time to edit and revise your composition. Your score will be based on your writing composition, not on your planning page.

GO ON ▶

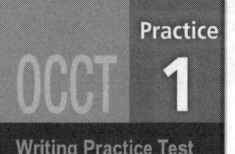

Name _____ Date _____

Planning Page

> Think about a time when you chose to work with others to complete a task. Describe that task and explain whether teamwork helped or hindered you.

In the space below, you may PLAN your composition. You might consider using a web, cluster, list, story map, or any other way to help you organize your writing. Do not write your final draft on this page. Any writing on this page will not be scored. Write your composition on the lined pages that follow.

GO ON ▶

Think about a time when you chose to work with others to complete a task. Describe that task and explain whether teamwork helped or hindered you.

Name _____ Date _____

Practice 1 — OCCT Writing Practice Test

Name _____ Date _____

Name _____ **Date** _____

DO NOT WRITE OUTSIDE THE BOX.

DO NOT WRITE OUTSIDE THE BOX.

GO ON ▶

Practice 1 — Writing Practice Test

Name _____ Date _____

DO NOT WRITE OUTSIDE THE BOX.

Practice OCCT 2 Reading Practice Test

Name _____ Date _____

OCCT Reading Practice Test 2

Here is a list with pictures to help you locate the selections in your Reading Practice Test. The questions follow each selection.

A Trip to the Aquarium .... Page 119

Inventing the Telephone .... Page 124

Hector's Big Game .... Page 129

The New Science of Sleep .... Page 136

Buying Alaska .... Page 141

Mystery Solved! .... Page 146

Writing Practice Test .... Page 152

GO ON ▶

OCCT Test Preparation   Page 118   Reading Practice Test

Read the selection below. Then answer the questions that follow.

A Trip to the Aquarium

1   Anna usually slept until the last possible minute, but today was different. Anna's mother came to wake her and found her already dressed and ready to go.

2   "What's going on?" asked her mother.

3   "Today's the field trip!" Anna exclaimed.

4   Mr. Giannaro's fourth-grade class was visiting the aquarium. Anna had been looking forward to this trip for months. She hoped to study the lives of fish and other sea creatures when she got older. She had seen TV shows that showed their underwater world. Today, though, would be her first chance to see these amazing animals for herself.

5   Everyone seemed excited about the special day, even Mr. Giannaro. He was wearing a tie with tiny pictures of whales. During the bus ride to the aquarium Anna told her seatmate, Angela, that she wanted to see the dolphins.

6   "I don't like big fish," said Angela. "I like angelfish."

7   "Dolphins aren't really fish. They breathe air," Anna explained. She described the tricks that they could do, but nothing she said persuaded Angela.

8   When the class arrived, Janet, a guide, greeted them. Janet took them to see many different tanks. First, they saw what looked like big flowers with fish swimming around them. Janet explained that the flowers were really animals. Then, they saw a tank filled with many brightly colored fish.

GO ON ▶

9 "Look at the angelfish!" exclaimed Angela.

10 After they had seen jellyfish, sea turtles, and strange-looking manta rays, Janet told the class that they had another surprise coming.

11 "We're going to see a seal show," Janet said. Anna frowned. She asked Janet whether they would also see the dolphins.

12 "You'll have to come back tomorrow to see them," said Janet. "Only the seals are performing today."

13 The seals put on a wonderful show. They jumped out of the water to catch fish. One of the seals jumped through a hoop. Then Janet got two seals to bounce a ball back and forth. The class clapped and laughed at the seals' tricks.

14 As the class went downstairs to eat lunch, Janet and Mr. Giannaro stopped Anna.

15 "I hear you're interested in life under water," Janet said.

16 "This is an amazing place!" Anna replied. "I only wish I could see the dolphins, too."

17 "Well, we'll have to leave pretty soon. But you can see the dolphins for a minute. Janet has offered to show them to you," Mr. Giannaro told her.

18 Janet brought Anna into the area where the dolphins were kept. She introduced Anna to the head dolphin trainer, Steve. Steve showed Anna the five dolphins and told her how they used sound to talk to each other under water. Then he gave her a small dolphin pin as a gift.

19 When she joined the rest of her class, Anna showed her pin proudly to Angela, who had a postcard with an angelfish on it.

20 "This is the best field trip ever," Anna thought happily.

1. The sentence "First, they saw what looked like big flowers with fish swimming around them" is an example of

- (A) a simile.
- B a metaphor.
- C a hyperbole.
- D personification.

2. Which word is an antonym for <u>arrived</u> as it used in this story?

- A asked
- B went
- C showed
- (D) left

3. Anna wakes up unusually early because

- A she needs to meet with Angela.
- B she is worried about the field trip.
- C she needs to stop being late to school.
- (D) she is excited about the trip to the Aquarium.

4 Why does Anna frown when she hears about the seal show?

A She is shy around strangers.
B She is afraid of seals.
C She wants to see the dolphins. *(circled)*
D She leaves her lunch on the bus.

5 In paragraph 18, <u>sound</u> means

A words.
B whistles.
C singing. *(circled)*
D whispers.

6 What happens <u>after</u> Janet brings Anna into the area where the dolphins are kept?

A Steve gives Anna a dolphin pin as a gift.
B Steve shows Janet the five dolphins. *(circled)*
C Anna shows her postcard to Angela.
D Anna introduces Janet to Steve.

7 What is Anna's main problem in the story?

A She usually sleeps until the last possible minute.

B Angela thinks that dolphins are fish.

C She will miss the dolphins' performance.

D The class must leave the aquarium soon.

8 Why is Anna interested in underwater life?

A She wants to study the lives of fish when she is older.

B She has visited many aquariums before.

C She wants to learn how to train dolphins.

D She likes to go fishing with her grandfather.

9 How are Anna and Angela alike?

A Both think that dolphins are fish.

B Both are excited to visit the aquarium.

C Both are curious to see the seals.

D Both sleep till the last minute.

STOP

Read the selection below. Then answer the questions that follow.

Inventing the Telephone

1   Suppose that you wanted to talk to your friend across the street without leaving your house. You could try yelling, but you would have to yell loudly. Also, that would be very rude. On the other hand, you could use a telephone to speak to your friend. You could even talk to someone on the other side of the planet with a telephone. Where did this powerful machine come from?

2   Today, telephones are a part of everyday life. But 150 years ago, no one had ever seen one. People who wanted to send messages over long distances used the telegraph. The telegraph used patterns of dots and dashes to send messages. Different patterns stood for the letters of the alphabet. Telegraph wires carried messages hundreds or even thousands of miles.

3   Alexander Graham Bell, who was born in Scotland, studied how the telegraph worked. From childhood, he was interested in sounds and human speech. His father was a well-known expert on speech, and his mother was unable to hear. As a young man, Bell worked as a teacher for deaf students. He worked in his spare time on his idea for a better telegraph.

4   Since more and more telegraph messages were being sent over telegraph wires, Bell wanted to create a new telegraph that could send many messages at the same time. Bell thought that his telegraph would use different pitches of sound to keep the various messages separate.

5   Bell worked with an assistant, Thomas Watson, to perfect his new telegraph. One day, while they worked on their project, Bell made an accidental discovery. He learned that electricity could carry sound directly. He decided to work on a machine that would carry the sound of a person's voice from one place to another.

6   Bell and Watson worked on the telephone for many months. Their basic idea was correct, but they were unable to make the sound easy to understand. On February 14, 1876, Bell announced to the U.S. government that he had found a way to carry the human voice over wires. But the world's first telephone call happened a few weeks later. Bell made the call on March 10 to his assistant, saying, "Mr. Watson, come here. I want you." That summer, he introduced his new invention to the world at the Philadelphia Centennial Exposition.

10

What invention in the story was invented <u>more</u> than 150 years ago?

A Bell telegraph
B cellular telephone
C Bell telephone
D electric telegraph *(circled)*

11

Which sentence is an opinion in the selection?

A Also, that would be very rude. *(circled)*
B Today, telephones are a part of everyday life.
C He learned that electricity could carry sound directly.
D Bell and Watson worked on the telephone for many months.

12

Why does the author give information about Alexander Graham Bell's parents?

A to point out that Bell was born in Europe
B to show that Bell needed help to invent the telephone
C to suggest why Bell was interested in speech and sound *(circled)*
D to question whether Bell had proper training as a teacher

13

Why did Bell want to invent a telegraph that could send many messages at once?

A The demand for telegraphs was growing quickly.
B Thomas Watson asked him to perfect the telegraph.
C Bell wanted to return to Scotland.
D A single pitch of sound could keep messages in order.

15

What is the most important fact that Bell learns by accident?

A Telegraphs send messages over wires.
B Electricity carries sound directly.
C Letters of the alphabet stand for sounds.
D Every voice has a different sound.

14

Which word means nearly the same as various?

A important
B simple
C loud
D different

16

A reader can tell that Bell had always been interested in sound and speech because he

A used to teach deaf students.
B used to be a musician.
C could speak many languages.
D studied electricity for a long time.

17

This article is mostly about

A the sound of human speech.
B the invention of a useful machine.
C the different kinds of telegraph wire.
D the childhood of Alexander Graham Bell.

18

Which word would a reader use to look for information about Bell in an encyclopedia?

A Alexander
B inventor
C telegraph
D Bell

Read the selection below. Then answer the questions that follow.

Hector's Big Game

1   Sixteen teams made up Newton's Double-A League. Only two had made it all the way to the championship game. One of them was Hector's team, the Badgers. The other team was the Jayhawks.

2   All season long, the Badgers and the Jayhawks had battled for first place. No other team came close. The two teams' record playing against each other had ended up dead even, with two wins on each side. Now Hector stood on the mound, about to throw the championship game's first pitch.

3   There was only one problem. Hector didn't want to be there.

4   He knew that his team could win. And he knew that he could lead them to victory. But his little brother Tony was not watching him today. He was at home with a fever. Hector's parents were home with him. Hector could tell that they were a little worried.

5   Hector wanted to be home with his brother, too. But Tony had persuaded him to play in today's game.

6   "You have worked too hard to quit now," Tony had said. "I'll be all right."

7   "Ball four!" the umpire yelled.

8   The first Jayhawk batter jogged to first base. Coach Freeman looked at Hector curiously. Hector had told the coach about his problem. But he had also promised to concentrate on the game, even though he had other things on his mind. What was the coach thinking now? Would he keep Hector in the game?

GO ON ▶

9   Eight innings later, Hector was still pitching. Both teams were playing as well as they had ever played. At first, the Jayhawks were winning. But Hector's team had slowly narrowed the lead. Then they pulled ahead by a single run. One more out and the championship was theirs. The Jayhawks had one runner on base. Their star hitter, Buck Turner, stepped to the plate.

10 Just then, Hector saw something from the corner of his eye.

11 It was Tony! He was sitting down in the bleachers, and Hector's parents were there, too! Hector <u>felt a huge weight lift off his chest.</u> He threw the pitch to Buck.

12 Buck hit a home run. The game was over.

13 Hector did not mind a bit. His brother was feeling better, and that was what really mattered. Then he saw Coach Freeman coming his way.

14 "I'm sorry, Coach," he said.

15 "No need to apologize, Hector," the coach replied. "You did your best today. I could not be more proud. Now go shake Buck Turner's hand."

GO ON ▶

19 The idiom "dead even" most nearly means

A fair.
B tied.
C exact.
D buried.

20 What does the phrase "felt a huge weight lift off his chest" mean?

A felt he could move more easily
B felt like something hit him hard
C felt like everybody was looking at him
D felt he did not have to worry anymore

21 What happens after Buck Turner comes to the plate?

A The Jayhawks win by one run.
B The game is a tie.
C The Badgers win by one run.
D The Badgers win by two runs.

22 Why does Hector tell Coach Freeman that he is sorry?

A Hector throws the losing pitch.
B Hector skips the championship game.
C Hector forgets to shake Buck Turner's hand.
D Hector forgets to tell the coach about his brother.

23 Which meaning of <u>coach</u> is used in paragraph 8?

A motorbus
B four-wheeled carriage
C sports trainer
D private teacher

24 What is Hector's <u>main</u> problem in the story?

A He is friends with the Jayhawks' star hitter.
B He has never played in an important game.
C He knows his parents are watching him.
D He is worried about his brother, who is at home sick.

OCCT Test Preparation — Page 132 — Reading Practice Test

GO ON ▶

25 How do Hector's feelings change in the story?

A from tired to strong
B from happy to sad
C from proud to mad
D from worried to glad

26 Which theme is found in "Hector's Big Game"?

A Play the game fairly rather than cheat.
B Listen to what adults have to say.
C Love your family more than winning.
D Concentrate on the game.

27 How was Hector's problem solved?

A His team lost the championship game.
B His family came to the championship game.
C His coach replaced him with another pitcher.
D He walked the first Jayhawks hitter.

GO ON ▶

28 How does Hector feel about losing to the Jawhawks?

A He is angry.
B He feels guilty.
C He is relieved.
D He does not mind.

29 A reader can tell this selection is fiction because the writer

A tells about imaginary characters.
B uses real people.
C uses short sentences.
D tells us about his own life.

30 Which sentence is a summary of paragraph 2?

A The Badgers were most likely to win the final.
B The finalist teams were both good.
C The championship had just started.
D The Jayhawks made it to the final out of luck.

GO ON ▶

31 Readers can tell that Coach Freeman is <u>not</u> upset about losing the game because

A he knows Hector did his best.
B he knows the Jayhawks were the stronger team.
C he knows the Badgers can still win the championship.
D he is happy that Tony is okay.

32 Which word <u>best</u> describes Tony?

A jealous
B brave
C considerate
D unhappy

33 A synonym for <u>concentrate</u> as used in paragraph 8 is

A agree.
B rely.
C insist.
D focus.

Read the selection below. Then answer the questions that follow.

The New Science of Sleep

1   Do you feel rested and alert right now? If you do not, then you have a lot of company. Recent studies suggest that most Americans sleep less than they should. Often people believe that getting by with less sleep is a sign of willpower. They could not be more wrong. Sleeping is an important part of a healthy lifestyle. You should plan your day to give yourself plenty of time to sleep.

2   Lack of sleep can lead to serious consequences. It can damage your health. Although no one is really sure why the body needs sleep, people who go without enough sleep for long periods begin to become weak and sick. The body has trouble fighting off disease when it is tired. For reasons that are not yet clear, people who sleep too little also tend to gain weight. One common response to being tired is overeating.

3   Sleep is not just important for your body. Your mind also needs enough rest every night. Scientists believe that sleeping and dreaming are necessary in order to form lasting memories. In one study, students who learned a new task were tested on it the next day. Those who slept for less than six hours performed as if they were relearning the task from the beginning. Only those who had slept for more than six hours showed that they remembered what they had learned. Sleep also affects your mood. People who need sleep often become angry, irritable, or depressed.

4   If you sleep too little, you may also become a danger to those around you. People who drive when they are drowsy are more likely to have accidents. Since sleepiness can lead to poor decision-making, people with jobs that can affect lives, such as doctors or airplane pilots, must be sure to get enough sleep.

5   Of course, once in a while everyone has a sleepless night. Taking a nap or catching up on your sleep the next night will help. But if you find yourself waking up tired and dragging yourself to school or work day after day, it is time to commit to a better sleep schedule.

6   Go to bed a little earlier every day for several days. Avoid too much activity right before bed. It's a good time to try reading. Before you know it, you will face the day fully rested. Getting the proper amount of sleep is not laziness. It is a smart, responsible thing to do.

34 Which is an opinion from the selection?

A Sleep also affects your mood.
B Your mind also needs enough rest every night.
C It is a smart, responsible thing to do.
D The body has trouble fighting off disease when it is tired.

35 In paragraph 3, <u>relearning</u> most nearly means

A learning with.
B learning through.
C learning again.
D learning for.

36 Which job is <u>most</u> dangerous after a sleepless night?

A journalist
B cartoonist
C truck driver
D gardener

GO ON ▶

37 A synonym for drowsy is

A upset.
B troubled.
C busy.
D) tired.

38 Why do doctors need to get enough sleep?

A Tired doctors are at high risk for depression.
B Tired doctors would set an unhealthy example.
C Tired doctors could make their patients sick.
D Tired doctors could make bad decisions.

39 What is the most important bedtime activity to help you sleep?

A eating
B reading
C talking
D walking

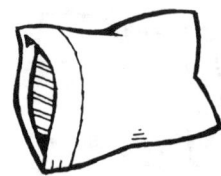

40 Which book would best help a student find information about the benefits of sleep?

A Sleeping for Health
B The Meaning of Dreams
C History of Beds from Ancient Egypt to Today
D Sleeping Outside: A Guide to Camping

41 What does the author suggest to the reader?

A Getting by with little sleep is a sign of willpower.
B Getting by with little sleep is bad for one's health.
C Getting by with little sleep is rare in the United States.
D Getting by with little sleep is better than sleeping too much.

42 The author wrote this selection mainly to

A tell readers how to lose weight.
B entertain readers with unusual facts.
C persuade readers to get enough sleep.
D inform readers that sleep cures diseases.

STOP

Read the selection below. Then answer the questions that follow.

Buying Alaska

1   Did you know that the state of Alaska used to be a part of the country of Russia? A narrow body of water separates Alaska from the eastern part of Russia. This body of water is called the Bering Strait. It is named for Vitus Bering, an explorer who visited Alaska. Soon after Bering's visit, fur trappers from Russia came to Alaska to live. The United States agreed that Russia had the right to own Alaska.

2   By the middle 1800s, Russia wanted to give up Alaska. The fur trade no longer made much money because the number of otters and seals had dropped. Meanwhile, Russia was fighting a war against England. The Russians found it difficult to defend Alaska. Eventually, the Russian government believed that Alaska had become too expensive to keep. The best solution seemed to be selling Alaska to the United States.

3   The Russians spoke with William Seward, an American official, about selling Alaska. Seward was in favor of the deal. The new President of the United States, Andrew Johnson, agreed as well. In October 1867, Seward made a deal with Russia to buy Alaska for $7.2 million. Although this was a great deal of money at the time, it was actually a good deal.

4   However, many Americans at the time believed that Seward's deal was a mistake. People nicknamed Alaska "Seward's Icebox" and "Seward's Folly." Few people showed interest in moving to Alaska. In 1880, fewer than 500 non-native settlers lived in Alaska. The United States' government paid little attention to its new property for almost 30 years.

5   All that changed when gold was discovered in Alaska. Thousands of people poured into the new territory in search of a quick fortune. Alaska's other natural resources, such as salmon and oil, were soon developed as well. By 1916, Alaskans asked the United States' government to admit Alaska as a state. In 1959, Alaska finally became the forty-ninth, and largest, state.

GO ON ▶

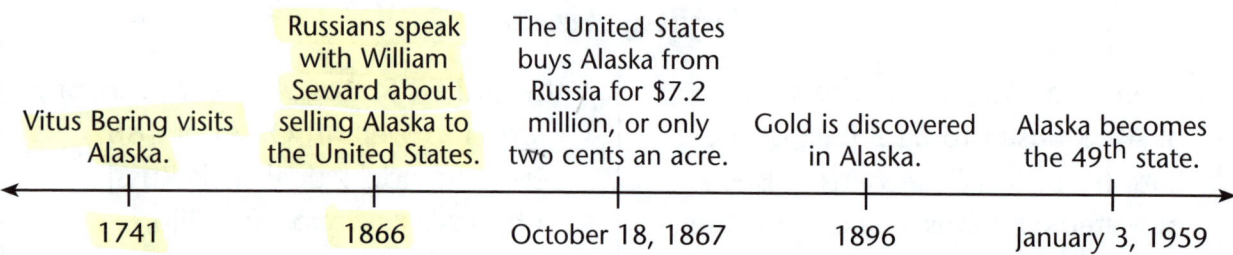

Vitus Bering visits Alaska.	Russians speak with William Seward about selling Alaska to the United States.	The United States buys Alaska from Russia for $7.2 million, or only two cents an acre.	Gold is discovered in Alaska.	Alaska becomes the 49th state.
1741	1866	October 18, 1867	1896	January 3, 1959

43

Based on the time line, when did Vitus Bering visit Alaska?

A 1741
B 1866
C 1867
D 1896

44

Based on the time line, what happened in 1866?

A Vitus Bering visited Alaska.
B Russia offered to sell Alaska.
C Gold was discovered in Alaska.
D The United States bought Alaska.

45

Why did Russia want to sell Alaska to the United States?

A Alaska was too far away from Russia.
B The United States threatened to fight Russia.
C Alaska had become too expensive for Russia.
D The United States wanted Alaska's gold.

GO ON ▶

46 What happened after March 1867 but before 1896?

A Russia offered to sell Alaska to the United States.
B Vitus Bering explored Alaska.
C People called Alaska "Seward's Folly."
D Alaska became the forty-ninth state.

47 Which meaning of poured is used in paragraph 5?

A rushed in a group
B put in a container
C rained very heavily
D said with feeling

48 In what way did Americans change their feelings about Alaska?

A At first they wanted Alaska to become a state, but later they thought buying Alaska was a mistake.
B At first they believed Alaska would make them rich, but later they called it "Seward's Folly."
C At first they wanted to move to Alaska, but later few decided to move there.
D At first they believed buying Alaska was a waste of money, but later they understood its value.

GO ON ▶

49 The author wrote this selection mainly to

A inform the reader about the history of Alaska.
B entertain the reader with a story about Alaska.
C persuade the reader to move to Alaska.
D tell the reader some of the nicknames for Alaska.

50 Which source would best help a student learn more about the search for gold in Alaska?

A a book of maps and charts of Alaska
B an article about the economy of Russia
C an encyclopedia article about gold
D an Internet site about the history of Alaska

51 After reading the title, "Buying Alaska," what question would the reader most likely ask?

A Was Alaska ever on sale?
B Where is Alaska located?
C What is Alaska famous for?
D When did Alaska become a state?

Read the selection below. Then answer the questions that follow.

Mystery Solved!

1   Katie looked around her room in a panic. Her eyes were as wide as if she had seen a ghost.

2   "Where could that scarf be?" she cried out.

3   The scarf was a gift for her grandmother. Katie had been saving money for a month to buy it. She knew that the scarf had been on her bed that morning. Someone must have stolen it!

4   "What's the problem, Katie?" Mr. McAdams stood at his daughter's door.

5   She told him about the missing scarf. He nodded.

6   "Katie, there's one sure way to find a thief. First, ask yourself who wanted that scarf. Then, ask yourself who was able to get to it. If anyone fits both descriptions, then you will have found your culprit."

7   The answer to the first question was simple. If anyone wanted to take that scarf away from her, it was her brother Jonah. He was always looking for ways to tease his younger sister, but there was a problem. Jonah spent last night at his friend's house and came home only a few moments ago. Could he have pulled off the theft so quickly?

8   She knocked on her brother's door.

9   "Who is it?" he called.

10 "Jonah, what did you do with my scarf?" Katie demanded.

GO ON ▶

11   He opened his door with a puzzled look. Her brother did not have the scarf. Katie felt guilty.

12   "I'm sorry for thinking you took my scarf," Katie said.

13   "That's OK," said Jonah.

14   Still searching to find the missing scarf, Katie thought about the second question. Besides herself, only one person had spent time in her room since yesterday. Her best friend Josie came over that morning to play. But Katie could not imagine that Josie had taken the scarf. Still, it was her only lead. She dialed Josie's number.

15   "What's up?" the familiar voice answered.

16   "Hi, Josie. Hey, what do you think of that scarf?"

17   "It is not my style, but I think it is perfect for your grandma."

18   Mr. McAdams came in as Katie was hanging up the phone.

19   "I'll never solve this mystery," she cried. "The only person who would have wanted the scarf was Jonah, and he could not have taken it. The only person who could have taken it was Josie, and she would not want it."

20   "Maybe you are overlooking someone," Mr. McAdams replied. Katie looked up and followed his gaze. He was looking at their cat, McWhiskers.

21   "Of course!" Katie said. "McWhiskers is always in my room, and he loves to play with cloth. I will bet the scarf is tucked away in his basket!"

22   That was exactly where Katie found it.

52 Why does Katie become upset over the missing scarf?

- A She wants to show the scarf to Josie.
- B She wants to tease her younger brother.
- C She wants to give the scarf to her grandmother.
- D She wants to wear the scarf for her grandmother.

53 In paragraph 6, <u>culprit</u> most nearly means

- A scarf.
- B thief.
- C friend.
- D brother.

54 What made Katie think that her brother took the scarf?

- A He likes to tease Katie.
- B He often takes Katie's things.
- C He is without a scarf of his own.
- D He plans to give the scarf to Katie.

GO ON

55 Why would Josie leave the scarf alone?

A She likes other kinds of scarves.
B She already has too many scarves.
C She cares for Katie as a good friend.
D She spends little time in Katie's room.

56 How are Josie and Jonah alike?

A Both want Katie's scarf.
B Both are related to Katie.
C Both were in Katie's room.
D Both are questioned by Katie.

57 How does Mr. McAdam help Katie solve her problem?

A He buys a new scarf for Katie's grandmother.
B He gives her advice about finding the thief.
C He calls her grandmother to explain the situation.
D He asks Jonah about the missing scarf.

GO ON ▶

58 Who is the last suspect that Katie thinks of?

A Mr. McAdams
B Josie
C McWhiskers
D Jonah

59 What is the theme of "Mystery Solved"?

A Think twice before you act.
B If you think you won't succeed, try again.
C Learn only using your eyes and ears.
D Know that it is better to give than to receive.

60 How are Josie and Jonah different?

A Jonah couldn't have taken the scarf while Josie could have.
B Josie took the scarf, while Jonah didn't.
C Jonah gave the scarf to the cat and Josie didn't
D Josie didn't give the scarf to her grandmother, while Jonah did.

STOP

ANSWER DOCUMENT

Name _____ Date _____

Practice 2 — OCCT Test Preparation

1. Ⓐ Ⓑ Ⓒ Ⓓ
2. Ⓐ Ⓑ Ⓒ Ⓓ
3. Ⓐ Ⓑ Ⓒ Ⓓ
4. Ⓐ Ⓑ Ⓒ Ⓓ
5. Ⓐ Ⓑ Ⓒ Ⓓ
6. Ⓐ Ⓑ Ⓒ Ⓓ
7. Ⓐ Ⓑ Ⓒ Ⓓ
8. Ⓐ Ⓑ Ⓒ Ⓓ
9. Ⓐ Ⓑ Ⓒ Ⓓ

10. Ⓐ Ⓑ Ⓒ Ⓓ
11. Ⓐ Ⓑ Ⓒ Ⓓ
12. Ⓐ Ⓑ Ⓒ Ⓓ
13. Ⓐ Ⓑ Ⓒ Ⓓ
14. Ⓐ Ⓑ Ⓒ Ⓓ
15. Ⓐ Ⓑ Ⓒ Ⓓ
16. Ⓐ Ⓑ Ⓒ Ⓓ
17. Ⓐ Ⓑ Ⓒ Ⓓ
18. Ⓐ Ⓑ Ⓒ Ⓓ

19. Ⓐ Ⓑ Ⓒ Ⓓ
20. Ⓐ Ⓑ Ⓒ Ⓓ
21. Ⓐ Ⓑ Ⓒ Ⓓ
22. Ⓐ Ⓑ Ⓒ Ⓓ
23. Ⓐ Ⓑ Ⓒ Ⓓ
24. Ⓐ Ⓑ Ⓒ Ⓓ
25. Ⓐ Ⓑ Ⓒ Ⓓ
26. Ⓐ Ⓑ Ⓒ Ⓓ
27. Ⓐ Ⓑ Ⓒ Ⓓ
28. Ⓐ Ⓑ Ⓒ Ⓓ
29. Ⓐ Ⓑ Ⓒ Ⓓ
30. Ⓐ Ⓑ Ⓒ Ⓓ
31. Ⓐ Ⓑ Ⓒ Ⓓ
32. Ⓐ Ⓑ Ⓒ Ⓓ
33. Ⓐ Ⓑ Ⓒ Ⓓ

34. Ⓐ Ⓑ Ⓒ Ⓓ
35. Ⓐ Ⓑ Ⓒ Ⓓ
36. Ⓐ Ⓑ Ⓒ Ⓓ
37. Ⓐ Ⓑ Ⓒ Ⓓ
38. Ⓐ Ⓑ Ⓒ Ⓓ
39. Ⓐ Ⓑ Ⓒ Ⓓ
40. Ⓐ Ⓑ Ⓒ Ⓓ
41. Ⓐ Ⓑ Ⓒ Ⓓ
42. Ⓐ Ⓑ Ⓒ Ⓓ

43. Ⓐ Ⓑ Ⓒ Ⓓ
44. Ⓐ Ⓑ Ⓒ Ⓓ
45. Ⓐ Ⓑ Ⓒ Ⓓ
46. Ⓐ Ⓑ Ⓒ Ⓓ
47. Ⓐ Ⓑ Ⓒ Ⓓ
48. Ⓐ Ⓑ Ⓒ Ⓓ
49. Ⓐ Ⓑ Ⓒ Ⓓ
50. Ⓐ Ⓑ Ⓒ Ⓓ
51. Ⓐ Ⓑ Ⓒ Ⓓ

52. Ⓐ Ⓑ Ⓒ Ⓓ
53. Ⓐ Ⓑ Ⓒ Ⓓ
54. Ⓐ Ⓑ Ⓒ Ⓓ
55. Ⓐ Ⓑ Ⓒ Ⓓ
56. Ⓐ Ⓑ Ⓒ Ⓓ
57. Ⓐ Ⓑ Ⓒ Ⓓ
58. Ⓐ Ⓑ Ⓒ Ⓓ
59. Ⓐ Ⓑ Ⓒ Ⓓ
60. Ⓐ Ⓑ Ⓒ Ⓓ

Name _____ Date _____

OCCT Writing Practice Test 2

Today you will write a composition on an assigned topic. Your writing will be scored on how fully you develop the topic and on how well you organize and express your ideas. Your composition will be scored by trained readers. As you work, keep in mind these three stages of the writing process:

- **Planning:** Take time to plan your writing by listing, outlining, or organizing your ideas in the space provided.

- **Writing:** Write about the topic in a clear and logical manner on the five lined pages following the *Planning Page*. You do not need to use all of the pages, but make sure your composition is as complete as possible. Be sure to include a beginning, a middle, and an ending for your composition.

- **Editing/Revising:** Take time to reread what you have written, and decide if you need to add more details or change the organization of your composition. At the same time, look for and correct any errors in grammar, punctuation, capitalization, and spelling. You may use the *Writer's Checklist* to help you revise your writing.

Most students will be able to complete the writing task within about 50 minutes, but you may take up to one extra hour to complete your test. Try to budget your time wisely so you will have time to edit and revise your composition. Your score will be based on your writing composition, not on your planning page.

GO ON ▶

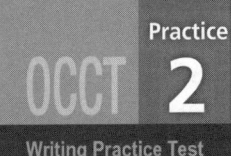

Name _____ Date _____

Planning Page

Think about a time when you had to solve a problem. Describe the problem and explain how you came up with a solution.

In the space below, you may PLAN your composition. You might consider using a web, cluster, list, story map, or any other way to help you organize your writing. Do not write your final draft on this page. Any writing on this page will not be scored. Write your composition on the lined pages that follow.

GO ON ▶

Name _____ Date _____

Think about a time when you had to solve a problem. Describe the problem and explain how you came up with a solution.

DO NOT WRITE OUTSIDE THE BOX.

OCCT Reading Practice Test 3

Here is a list with pictures to help you locate the selections in your Reading Test Book. The questions follow each selection.

 The Perfect Deer Family ....Page 160

 Power from Wind and Water ....Page 165

 My Own Voice ....Page 170

 Martin Luther King Jr.:
More Than a Man with a Dream ....Page 175

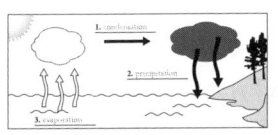 Sea Star ....Page 180

 The Water Cycle ....Page 183

 Lisbeth's Writing Plan....................................Page 188

Facing Fear...Page 190

Writing Practice Test ....Page 194

GO ON ▶

The Perfect Deer Family
by Mary DiMenna

1   Long ago, a deer family lived in the forest. They were the biggest, fastest animals in the forest. They were also very beautiful. They thought that they were better than all of the other animals in the forest. In fact, they thought they were perfect.

2   One day, Mr. Perfect Deer was feeling especially proud. He said, "We are so beautiful with our lovely smooth skin and splendid ears. We can run like the wind. We should have all of the land in the forest for ourselves!"

3   Small Perfect Deer and Smaller Perfect Deer quickly agreed. Even Mrs. Perfect Deer liked the idea.

4   The Perfect Deer family went to work. They chased away all of the other animals. They painted and erected little signs that said "Perfect Deer Only." Each day they marked out a larger and larger circle in the forest.

5   As their circle grew bigger, the Perfect Deer family members congratulated one another on their plan. They thought that they were both beautiful and smart.

6   Each day, however, the deer had to do more and more work to keep the other animals out. Instead of playing hide-and-seek all day, Small Deer and Smaller Deer had to make

sure that no other animals stepped on their land. After a few weeks, Mrs. Perfect Deer had to help, too.

7   By the time a month had passed, even Mr. Perfect Deer had to spend his whole day protecting their land. That made him cranky.

8   There were other problems, too. One night Smaller Deer said, "I miss the sound of the birds chirping in the trees every morning."

9   Small Deer added in a grumpy voice, "I don't have anyone to play soccer with anymore. And there's nobody my age to talk to!"

10 Mrs. Perfect Deer sighed, "I miss Honey Raccoon. We used to share such good stories."

11 Even Mr. Perfect Deer saw that the new plan had its drawbacks. He grumbled, "I haven't had a good nap for weeks."

12 No one said anything more, but the decision was made. The next day, Small Deer pulled up the "Perfect Deer Only" signs. Mrs. Perfect Deer moved the family's house back toward the center of the circle.

13 Soon, Mr. Perfect Deer stopped guarding the land. Instead, he could be seen napping happily under the pines. Gradually, the other animals returned to all of the land in the forest. The Perfect Deer family was very glad to see and hear them.

GO ON ▶

Practice 3 — OCCT Reading Practice Test

Name _____ Date _____

1

The idiom "run like the wind" most nearly means run

A through the trees.
B slowly.
C when it's breezy.
D very fast.

2

What is the first event in the story that tells you that the plan for taking all of the land might not be a perfect plan?

A The Perfect Deer family must chase away all of the other animals.
B The Perfect Deer family must make a larger and larger circle.
C The Perfect Deer must do more and more work to keep other animals out.
D Mr. Perfect Deer must help his family keep other animals out.

3

In the story, which word has nearly the same meaning as chirping?

A singing
B eating
C flying
D playing

GO ON ▶

OCCT Test Preparation   Page 162   Reading Practice Test

4 Which word means nearly the opposite of grumpy?

A quiet
B cheerful
C loud
D helpful

5 What happens after Mr. Perfect Deer complains about missing his naps but before all of the other animals return to the forest?

A Mrs. Perfect Deer moves the family's home back.
B Small Deer misses playing soccer with his friends.
C Smaller Deer misses hearing the birds in the morning.
D Mr. Perfect Deer pulls up the "Perfect Deer Only" signs.

6 In what way did Mr. Perfect Deer change his mind about owning all of the land in the forest?

A At first he thought he would miss the other animals, but later he liked living without them.
B At first he thought that owning all of the land was a bad idea, but later he knew it was a good idea.
C At first he thought it would make his family happy, but later he found that it made his family unhappy.
D At first he thought he should share the land, but later he wanted to have all the land for himself.

GO ON ▶

Name _____ **Date** _____

7. Why does Small Deer pull up the "Perfect Deer Only" signs?

A to get more land for the Deer family

B to keep the other animals off the land

C to hear more of Honey Raccoon's stories

D to show that the other animals could return

8. Why did Mr. Perfect Deer nap happily under the pines?

A His family was fast, beautiful, and perfect.

B His family had stopped guarding their land.

C Small Deer was keeping the other animals away.

D The other animals had moved away from the forest.

9. In the story, what does the word underlined erected mean?

A cut out

B took down

C put up

D looked at

10. Which sentence best tells what the story is about?

A Members of the Perfect Deer family discover that they need more land.

B Members of the Perfect Deer family are big, fast, beautiful, and perfect.

C The Perfect Deer family finds that it is too much work to guard their land.

D The Perfect Deer family learns that being selfish can make them very lonely.

STOP

Power from Wind and Water

by José Pacheco

1   In the United States, we depend on fossil fuels—fuels that are formed in the earth from plant and animal remains—for most of our energy needs. Fossil fuels include coal and oil, which release harmful gases into the air when burned. We burn them to heat our homes and to run our cars. We also burn them to make electricity. We use electricity for lighting, heating, and making most machines run.

2   We do not have to depend on fossil fuels to make all of our electrical power, however. We can also get energy from water and wind. Both wind and water are *renewable* energy sources. Renewable means that we will not use them up because we do not burn them or destroy them to get power from them.

3   Moving water contains energy. We can turn this energy into electricity. One way to do this is by building dams. Dams are strong walls that hold back large amounts of water or control how much water flows in a particular place. When water that has been allowed to collect behind the wall finally gets high enough to go over the dam, it falls with great power. The farther it falls and the more of it there is, the more speed and energy the water has. The powerful moving water runs through pipes to a power station. It makes motors spin inside the power station. The motors then make electricity.

4   Although waterpower does not pollute the environment, it can have some bad effects. For example, dams can disturb fish by changing their habitats, sometimes causing fish to die. Dams can also put some dry land under water, affecting the habitats of other plants and animals.

5   Wind power is another clean way of making electricity. Getting energy from wind does not pollute the air.

6   We can get power from the wind in much the same way that we get power from water. Wind can make electricity because it is moving. Moving air turns the blades of wind machines. The blades are connected to a drive shaft, which is a long pole that spins when the blades turn. They are like windmills. The drive shaft then powers a generator. This generator makes electricity.

7   People often build wind farms, which are places where many wind machines are used together to create energy. Some of the best wind farms are on open, flat land. Others are at the tops of hills or near seashores.

Read the chart below to compare some basic facts about water and wind power.

Wind Power and Waterpower

How They Are the Same	How They Are Different
Wind and water are renewable forms of energy. We will not run out of them.	We now use about 15 times more energy from water than energy from wind.
Wind and water can produce electricity.	Water accounts for $\frac{3}{4}$ of the all the renewable energy we use. Wind accounts for less than $\frac{1}{15}$.

Source of Facts: United States Department of Energy

GO ON ▶

11 Wind power is compared to waterpower because **both**

A are made by dams with strong walls.

B are easy to create from their materials.

C come from burning fossil fuels.

D come from renewable energy sources.

12 What does the word **habitats** mean?

A homes

B water

C lives

D power

13 Which words from the story have almost the **same** meaning?

A fuel, water

B habitats, sources

C dam, farm

D power, energy

Name _____ **Date** _____

14

What is the first step in making electricity from wind?

A Moving air turns blades.

B Blades turn a drive shaft.

C A blade turns a generator.

D A drive shaft powers a generator.

15

Based on the chart, most of our renewable energy comes from

A wind.

B farms.

C water.

D electricity.

16

Based on the chart, both waterpower and wind power

A supply the same percent of our energy for electricity.

B are renewable fossil fuels that can make electricity.

C provide equal amounts of energy for making electricity.

D are renewable forms of energy that can make electricity.

GO ON ▶

17 This article is *mostly* about

A building walls for dams.

B getting power from fossil fuels.

C using water and wind for fuel.

D making wind farms on open land.

18 What was the author's purpose in writing "Power from Wind and Water"?

A to teach the reader how to build strong and tall dams

B to persuade readers to build wind farms on hilltops

C to explain why fossil fuels are a good source of energy

D to tell the reader about renewable forms of energy

Read the selection below. Then answer the questions that follow.

My Own Voice

by Melissa Hoffman

1   I was putting the finishing touches on my paper for our school's "My Most Memorable Person" writing contest when Lily called. "Are you done yet, Melissa?" she asked.

2   "Almost. I feel super about it, too. I wrote about Grandpa Scott, and it was as easy as drinking water. I just remembered what a strange but <u>likeable</u> guy he was, and my paper just about wrote itself!"

3   "Great," said Lily. "Mine was pretty easy, too. I wrote about Richard Thorpe."

4   "Richard Thorpe?" I asked. The name sounded familiar, but I did not know why.

5   "Yeah, our mayor!" Lily said. "Dad worked with him on the city planning project, so he gave me the idea."

6   "Oh," I said, and then there was a long pause. I had been kind of hoping to win the contest. However, who was Grandpa Scott when compared with the mayor of Springdale?

7   I recovered though. I asked Lily, "How did you come up with stuff to write about?"

8   Lily giggled nervously. She said, "Well, Dad just knew everything, and he stood over my shoulder when I wrote. He had lots of good ideas and big words!"

9   Oh," I said again, feeling a little more upset. Then I said, "I think I hear my mother calling." Actually, I was really just wishing she were calling so I could get off the phone.

10   The next day, our teacher Mr. Borrega said we were doing

GO ON

something new for the contest this year. Instead of just handing our papers in, everyone had to read them aloud. He would record us, and then the judges could hear how the papers sounded in our own voices.

11   I listened eagerly as the first few students read their papers. Some students had not tried very hard, but many had written pretty good papers. Still, I thought that they had not put in the "brave, bold words" and "sensory language" that Mr. Borrega was always talking about. I felt I had them all beat to pencil shavings until Lily got up to read.

12   As soon as she started to read, I got nervous. She talked about the "man for all seasons" and the "leader for the twenty-first century." She used many words that I did not understand. I worried that they were the big, bold words that Mr. Borrega really wanted. But then something odd happened. Lily mispronounced one of the words she had written. She turned red, but I was glad that she continued reading to the end of her essay.

13   Soon it was my turn. I could feel my voice fill up with pride as I read about Grandpa Scott. Proudly, I read out my big, brave, original descriptions. For example, I said that his heart was as big as a football stadium. I said that he had an appetite the size of Arizona. I said that, at first, he was as friendly as a package of frozen lima beans, but that he thawed out nicely after a while. I could tell by the way that the class listened that Grandpa was a pretty good topic after all.

14   When we were all finished reading our papers, Mr. Borrega said that he wished us all luck, especially those who had written in voices that were all our own. He looked straight at me when he said that. At that moment, I thought Grandpa would be as proud of me as a hen that laid a giant egg.

GO ON ▶

19

In the story, what does the word likeable mean?

A easily liked
B liked again
C liked by few
D never liked

20

What is the most important lesson that Melissa learns in the story?

A Always try hard to write your best.
B Always use your own ideas and words.
C Always read your writing aloud with feeling.
D Always know how to say the words.

21

If pronounced means "said correctly," what does mispronounced mean?

A said loudly
B said incorrectly
C said correctly again
D said correctly before

22

What happened after Lily told Melissa her topic but before Lily read her paper aloud?

A Melissa read her own paper aloud to the class.
B Mr. Borrega talked about writing in your own voice.
C Melissa said that her own paper had been easy to write.
D Mr. Borrega said that he would record students as they read aloud.

GO ON

23 In what way did Melissa change her mind about the topic for the contest?

A At first she thought that Richard Thorpe was a bad topic, but later she knew that he was a good topic.

B At first she thought that the mayor was a better topic than her grandpa, but later she knew that her grandpa was the better topic.

C At first she thought that her grandpa was a better topic than the mayor, but later she knew that the mayor was the better topic.

D At first she thought that Mr. Borrega was a bad topic, but later she knew that he was a good topic.

24 What is the first event in the story that shows Melissa is uneasy about her topic?

A Melissa thinks that Lily's topic is better than hers.

B Melissa wants to end her phone conversation with Lily.

C Melissa turns a bright shade of red while reading her paper aloud.

D Melissa announces how easy it was to write about Grandpa Scott.

25 How does Melissa change in the story?

A At first she is quiet; then she is loud.

B At first she is happy; then she is sad.

C At first she is surprised; then she is pleased.

D At first she is worried; then she is confident.

26 Why does Melissa compare her grandpa's heart to a football stadium?

A A football stadium is shaped like a heart.

B A football stadium is important to her grandpa.

C Like a football stadium, her grandpa's heart is big.

D Like a football stadium, her grandpa's heart is noisy.

27 Why does Mr. Borrega look at Melissa when he talks about writing in your own voice?

A He wants Melissa to win the writing contest.

B He knows that Melissa wrote in her own voice.

C He wants Melissa to get a good grade on the paper.

D He thinks that Melissa's paper used someone else's words.

28 A person who is "as friendly as a package of frozen lima beans"

A is unfriendly.

B enjoys lima beans.

C is friendly.

D is friendly, but cold all the time.

Read the selection below. Then answer the questions that follow.

Martin Luther King Jr.: More Than a Man with a Dream
by Brendan Nagle

1   Many people in the United States know a little bit about Martin Luther King Jr. Most people know that he was a leader of the civil rights movement. They have also heard that he gave a famous speech called "I Have a Dream." These two familiar facts are important. Yet, there is so much more to know about this great leader.

2   Martin Luther King Jr. was born in Atlanta, Georgia. He grew up in a neighborhood called Sweet Auburn. Only African Americans lived there. King's father was the minister of a church in Sweet Auburn.

3   Young Martin had a good childhood. His father had a great influence on him. He helped turn his son into a powerful public speaker. In his neighborhood, young Martin lived near the rich and the poor. He saw how laws that kept African Americans separate from white people affected their lives.

4   King went to school in the North. As a student, he learned about the theories of Mohandas Gandhi. Gandhi was from India, a country in Asia. Gandhi used peaceful means to cause his country to change. King admired Gandhi's peaceful way

GO ON ▶

because King believed that violence was not needed. Gandhi's ideas were like a road map that helped King find his own way.

5   When King returned to the South, some people in Montgomery, Alabama, asked him to lead their struggle. They were about to boycott the public buses in that city. That means they would refuse to ride them. Once Martin Luther King Jr. stepped forward to lead them, he never stopped being a leader. People believed in him and in his ideas.

6   During the most intense struggle for civil rights, people turned to Dr. King. He led marches. He addressed government leaders. He worked to get schools to teach all students together, and not to separate students because of the color of their skin. He worked for voting rights for African Americans. He worked to end laws and attitudes that were unfair. Although he preached love and peace, he also preached determination. He told people never to give up their struggle for justice. People of all races were inspired by his words and by his actions. They took courage from his courage.

7   People all over the world honored Dr. King. Although he received many awards and prizes, including the Nobel Peace Prize, Dr. King wanted to be remembered for helping people.

29 What happened <u>after</u> King's childhood but <u>before</u> he led the bus boycott?

A King learned about Gandhi.
B King preached determination.
C King worked for voting rights.
D King won the Nobel Peace Prize.

30 In the article, what does <u>peaceful</u> mean?

A able to have peace
B needing peace
C full of peace
D without peace

31 Why are Gandhi's ideas compared to a road map?

A because both can show distances and directions
B because both can show the way to go
C because both helped King travel to cities
D because both helped King change the world

GO ON ▶

32
What happened to make King a leader?

A People asked him to lead a boycott of public buses.

B He worked for voting rights for African Americans.

C People asked him to address government leaders.

D He worked for better schools for African Americans.

33
In the article, what does the word determination mean?

A looking for a purpose

B making a decision

C staying strong

D finding answers

34
What happened to make people follow King?

A He gave his "I Have a Dream" speech.

B He inspired people with words and actions.

C He grew up in an African American neighborhood.

D He was a student at a school in the North.

GO ON ▶

OCCT Test Preparation — Page 178 — Reading Practice Test

35

Why did the author write the article "Martin Luther King Jr.: More Than a Man with a Dream"?

A to teach readers about the civil rights movements

B to tell readers about the life of Martin Luther King Jr.

C to explain why the civil rights movement needed a leader

D to persuade readers to admire Martin Luther King Jr.

36

In this article, the word <u>theories</u> most nearly means

A ideas.

B creations.

C stories.

D travels.

37

What is the main idea of "Martin Luther King Jr.: More Than a Man with a Dream"?

A The speech "I Have a Dream" was what started the civil rights movement.

B Martin Luther King Jr. should be remembered for his life of service.

C The speech "I Have a Dream" was the most important thing that King did.

D Martin Luther King Jr. should be remembered for acting like Mohandas Gandhi.

Read the selection below. Then answer the questions that follow.

Sea Star
by Desiya Peterson

1 The sea star crawls over the land.
   Could it have five arms but not
   one hand?

   It is a star of the ocean,
5 A wonder of the sea.
   It is a spiny-skinned creature,
   A stanza of poetry.

   The sea star has a mouth, but it
   has no head.
10 Does it push its stomach from its
   mouth to be fed?

   It is a star of the ocean,
   A wonder of the sea.
   It is a unique creature,
15 A page out of a fantasy.

   One day a <u>predator</u> eats the sea
   star's arm.
   How can the sea star grow it back
   without a sign of harm?

20 It is a star of the ocean,
   A wonder of the sea.
   It is a strange creature,
   A chapter from a mystery.

GO ON ▶

38 Why does the sea star push its stomach out of its mouth?

A to eat its food
B to walk on land
C to grow back arms
D to swim in the ocean

39 In the poem, what does <u>predator</u> mean?

A a sea creature that is like the sea star
B an animal that hunts other animals
C a sea creature that is a stanza of poetry
D an animal with five arms and one hand

40 Why is the sea star compared to a chapter from a mystery?

A because both can be described
B because both can be about the sea
C because both are long and involved
D because both are strange and puzzling

GO ON ▶

41 Based on the illustration, you know that the sea star

A has five arms.
B crawls on land.
C regrows body parts.
D swims in the ocean.

42 The author says that the sea star is a "star of the ocean" because it

A lights up the water.
B crawls across the land.
C is an amazing creature.
D is a scary creature.

43 Why did the author write "Sea Star"?

A to teach readers about fantasy and mystery
B to persuade readers to collect sea stars
C to explain how sea stars and poetry are alike
D to entertain readers with a look at sea stars

44 What is the main idea of "Sea Star"?

A The sea star is an odd and scary sea creature.
B The sea star is a creature that has five arms but no hands.
C The sea star is a creature that can grow new body parts.
D The sea star is a strange and wonderful sea creature.

1. condensation
2. precipitation
3. evaporation

Read the selection below. Then answer the questions that follow.

The Water Cycle
by Marsha Boyle

1   Water is always on the move. The diagram above shows how water is always changing and flowing.

2   Water exists in different ways. It can be a liquid, like the water we drink. It can also be a gas. In this condition, water is called water vapor. The water cycle involves changes in the state of water.

3   One step in the water cycle is condensation. Condensation occurs when water vapor changes into a liquid. When water is a gas in the air and gets cold, it condenses. The condensed water forms clouds.

4   Next, more water vapor condenses. When the air and the clouds become too full and can no longer hold the water vapor, precipitation occurs. Precipitation is moisture falling to the earth. Precipitation is rain, snow, hail, or sleet.

5   When precipitation reaches the surface of the earth, some of it soaks into the ground. Some of it also goes into the oceans, lakes, or rivers. The water does not stay in the ground or in the bodies of water. That is because the sun plays a role in the water cycle.

6   The sun heats up the water. The heat makes the water turn into steam, or vapor. The vapor goes

GO ON

into the air. This process is called evaporation. Can you see the word <u>vapor</u> within the word <u>evaporation</u>?

7   After the water evaporates, it condenses. Then the water cycle starts all over again. That is why it is called a cycle. Like the wheels on a bicycle, a cycle is something that goes around and around. Unlike the wheels on a bicycle, though, the water cycle never stops.

8   Water recycles itself by means of the water cycle. This is one reason why we do not use up water. Water is always flowing away from the earth and back to earth again.

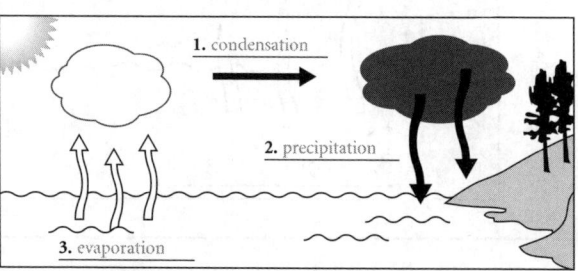

GO ON ▶

Diagram: Water cycle showing:
1. condensation
2. precipitation
3. evaporation

45. If vapor means gas, what does evaporation mean?

A the change from gas to liquid
B the condition of being a liquid
C the change from liquid to gas
D the condition of being a solid

46. Based on the diagram and the article, what happens after water is condensed in clouds?

A It turns into a gas called vapor.
B It turns into a solid that is heavy.
C It creates lakes and rivers on earth.
D It falls to the earth as precipitation.

47. Based on the article and the diagram, what happens to some water in lakes and oceans?

A It freezes into a solid.
B It causes precipitation.
C It causes condensation.
D It evaporates into the air.

GO ON ▶

The Water Cycle

1. condensation
2. precipitation
3. evaporation

48. What is the main idea of "The Water Cycle"?

A Water is always flowing and changing states.
B After water condenses, it falls as precipitation.
C The sun causes many changes in the water cycle.
D A cycle is something that goes around and around.

49. Based on the diagram, what happens first as a result of condensation?

A Rain falls.
B Clouds form.
C Ice forms.
D Water evaporates.

50. Based on the diagram, where does water go first when it evaporates?

A into the sun
B into the air
C into the ocean
D into the rain

OCCT Practice 3 — Reading Practice Test

Name _____ Date _____

1. condensation
2. precipitation
3. evaporation

51 Why is the water cycle compared to the wheels of a bicycle?

A because both go around
B because both never stop
C because both are not used up
D because both are necessary

52 What was the author's purpose in writing the article "The Water Cycle"?

A To entertain readers with a story about water
B To educate readers about an important scientific concept
C To explain how precipitation happens
D To show that water is necessary for life

Read the selection below. Then answer the questions that follow.

Lisbeth's Writing Plan

Main Idea: Pretty to Look At
Detail: long, white hair
Detail: big green eyes

Main Idea: A Mind of Her Own
Detail: does not come when called
Detail: loves her cat toys

Topic: Our Cat, Fluffy

Main Idea: Better Than a Bird
Detail: can be loud
Detail: need to be in a cage

Main Idea: Has Favorite Things
Detail: loves the big, red chair
Detail: likes anything that rolls

GO ON ▶

53 Which main idea is off topic and should be taken out of "Lisbeth's Writing Plan"?

A Pretty to Look At
B A Mind of Her Own
C Better Than a Bird
D Has Favorite Things

54 Based on the information in "Lisbeth's Writing Plan," what kind of paper is Lisbeth planning to write?

A a paper that tells a story about Fluffy
B a paper that persuades people to have cats as pets
C a paper that explains what Fluffy is like
D a paper that describes Fluffy's favorite places

55 Which idea in "Lisbeth's Writing Plan" should be moved because it is out of place?

A has long, white hair
B loves her cat toys
C loves the big, red chair
D likes anything that rolls

Read the selection below. Then answer the questions that follow.

Facing Fear

1   Carlos stared at the roller coaster as it sped along the track. His class was spending the day at the amusement park. Carlos liked the smaller rides, but he was scared of the idea of riding the roller coaster. His classmates rushed toward the line for the ride yelling for him to join them. Carlos could not get his mind off his fear.

2   Luc waved to Carlos. "The roller coaster looks scarier than it is," she said. "Besides, I will ride with you. There is a seat belt and safety bar to keep you safe."

3   Suddenly, Carlos felt better. "Thanks, Luc," he said, "I think I will ride the roller coaster." He ran ahead to get in line. Luc smiled and ran with him.

56 What is Carlos's <u>main</u> problem?

A He wants Luc to talk to him.
B He doesn't want to wait in line.
C He is worried about the class trip.
D He is scared of riding the roller coaster.

58 With which sentence would Carlos <u>most likely</u> agree?

A You should not go on field trips.
B It is okay to be afraid of things.
C All rides are scary and dangerous.
D You should always face your fears.

57 How is Carlos's problem solved?

A He runs with his classmates.
B Luc helps him get over his fear.
C He thinks about the seat belts and safety bar.
D His classmates decide not to ride the roller coaster.

GO ON ▶

59 How does Carlos change during the selection?

A At first he is scared, and then he has fun.

B At first he rushed to the ride, and then he changed his mind.

C At first Luc asks him to go with her, and then Carlos wants to go by himself.

D At first Carlos feels scared, and then he feels even more scared.

60 Which sentence states an opinion?

A "There is a safety belt to keep you safe."

B Carlos could not get his mind off his fear.

C "The roller coaster looks scarier than it is."

D He ran ahead to get in line.

STOP

ANSWER DOCUMENT

Name _____ Date _____

Practice 3 — OCCT Test Preparation

1. Ⓐ Ⓑ Ⓒ Ⓓ
2. Ⓐ Ⓑ Ⓒ Ⓓ
3. Ⓐ Ⓑ Ⓒ Ⓓ
4. Ⓐ Ⓑ Ⓒ Ⓓ
5. Ⓐ Ⓑ Ⓒ Ⓓ
6. Ⓐ Ⓑ Ⓒ Ⓓ
7. Ⓐ Ⓑ Ⓒ Ⓓ
8. Ⓐ Ⓑ Ⓒ Ⓓ
9. Ⓐ Ⓑ Ⓒ Ⓓ
10. Ⓐ Ⓑ Ⓒ Ⓓ

11. Ⓐ Ⓑ Ⓒ Ⓓ
12. Ⓐ Ⓑ Ⓒ Ⓓ
13. Ⓐ Ⓑ Ⓒ Ⓓ
14. Ⓐ Ⓑ Ⓒ Ⓓ
15. Ⓐ Ⓑ Ⓒ Ⓓ
16. Ⓐ Ⓑ Ⓒ Ⓓ
17. Ⓐ Ⓑ Ⓒ Ⓓ
18. Ⓐ Ⓑ Ⓒ Ⓓ

19. Ⓐ Ⓑ Ⓒ Ⓓ
20. Ⓐ Ⓑ Ⓒ Ⓓ
21. Ⓐ Ⓑ Ⓒ Ⓓ
22. Ⓐ Ⓑ Ⓒ Ⓓ
23. Ⓐ Ⓑ Ⓒ Ⓓ
24. Ⓐ Ⓑ Ⓒ Ⓓ
25. Ⓐ Ⓑ Ⓒ Ⓓ
26. Ⓐ Ⓑ Ⓒ Ⓓ
27. Ⓐ Ⓑ Ⓒ Ⓓ
28. Ⓐ Ⓑ Ⓒ Ⓓ

29. Ⓐ Ⓑ Ⓒ Ⓓ
30. Ⓐ Ⓑ Ⓒ Ⓓ
31. Ⓐ Ⓑ Ⓒ Ⓓ
32. Ⓐ Ⓑ Ⓒ Ⓓ
33. Ⓐ Ⓑ Ⓒ Ⓓ
34. Ⓐ Ⓑ Ⓒ Ⓓ
35. Ⓐ Ⓑ Ⓒ Ⓓ
36. Ⓐ Ⓑ Ⓒ Ⓓ
37. Ⓐ Ⓑ Ⓒ Ⓓ

38. Ⓐ Ⓑ Ⓒ Ⓓ
39. Ⓐ Ⓑ Ⓒ Ⓓ
40. Ⓐ Ⓑ Ⓒ Ⓓ
41. Ⓐ Ⓑ Ⓒ Ⓓ
42. Ⓐ Ⓑ Ⓒ Ⓓ
43. Ⓐ Ⓑ Ⓒ Ⓓ
44. Ⓐ Ⓑ Ⓒ Ⓓ

45. Ⓐ Ⓑ Ⓒ Ⓓ
46. Ⓐ Ⓑ Ⓒ Ⓓ
47. Ⓐ Ⓑ Ⓒ Ⓓ
48. Ⓐ Ⓑ Ⓒ Ⓓ
49. Ⓐ Ⓑ Ⓒ Ⓓ
50. Ⓐ Ⓑ Ⓒ Ⓓ
51. Ⓐ Ⓑ Ⓒ Ⓓ
52. Ⓐ Ⓑ Ⓒ Ⓓ

53. Ⓐ Ⓑ Ⓒ Ⓓ
54. Ⓐ Ⓑ Ⓒ Ⓓ
55. Ⓐ Ⓑ Ⓒ Ⓓ

56. Ⓐ Ⓑ Ⓒ Ⓓ
57. Ⓐ Ⓑ Ⓒ Ⓓ
58. Ⓐ Ⓑ Ⓒ Ⓓ
59. Ⓐ Ⓑ Ⓒ Ⓓ
60. Ⓐ Ⓑ Ⓒ Ⓓ

Name _____ Date _____

OCCT Writing Practice Test 3

Today you will write a composition on an assigned topic. Your writing will be scored on how fully you develop the topic and on how well you organize and express your ideas. Your composition will be scored by trained readers. As you work, keep in mind these three stages of the writing process:

- **Planning:** Take time to plan your writing by listing, outlining, or organizing your ideas in the space provided.

- **Writing:** Write about the topic in a clear and logical manner on the five lined pages following the *Planning Page*. You do not need to use all of the pages, but make sure your composition is as complete as possible. Be sure to include a beginning, a middle, and an ending for your composition.

- **Editing/Revising:** Take time to reread what you have written, and decide if you need to add more details or change the organization of your composition. At the same time, look for and correct any errors in grammar, punctuation, capitalization, and spelling. You may use the *Writer's Checklist* to help you revise your writing.

Most students will be able to complete the writing task within about 50 minutes, but you may take up to one extra hour to complete your test. Try to budget your time wisely so you will have time to edit and revise your composition. Your score will be based on your writing composition, not on your planning page.

GO ON

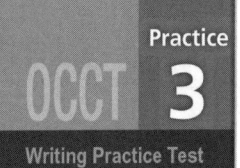

Name _____ Date _____

Planning Page

> Most people have a favorite sport, hobby, or after-school activity. Think about your favorite thing to do. Write a composition that explains why you like your favorite sport, hobby, or after-school activity.

In the space below, you may PLAN your composition. You might consider using a web, cluster, list, story map, or any other way to help you organize your writing. Do not write your final draft on this page. Any writing on this page will not be scored. Write your composition on the lined pages that follow.

GO ON ▶

OCCT Practice 3 Writing Practice Test

Name _____ Date _____

Most people have a favorite sport, hobby, or after-school activity. Think about your favorite thing to do. Write a composition that explains why you like your favorite sport, hobby, or after-school activity.

DO NOT WRITE OUTSIDE THE BOX.

OCCT Practice 3 Writing Practice Test

Name _____ Date _____

DO NOT WRITE OUTSIDE THE BOX.

Name _____ **Date** _____

DO NOT WRITE OUTSIDE THE BOX.